CW00952017

LIFE ON THE
Ramona
COASTER

RAMONA SINGER

POST HILL PRESS

A POST HILL PRESS BOOK
ISBN: 978-1-61868-876-7
ISBN (eBook): 978-1-61868-875-0

LIFE ON THE RAMONA COASTER

Cover Design by Ryan Truso
Cover Image by Bethany Michaela Photo

This is a work of nonfiction. Events, locales, and conversations are reconstructed from the author's memory. These stories have been retold as faithfully as possible, but all stories are those of the author and as such may be subject to discrepancies in details from actual events. However, in all cases, the author has attempted to assure that the essence of events and dialogue are as accurate as possible.

Post Hill Press
275 Madison Avenue, 14th Floor
New York, NY 10016
http://posthillpress.com

CONTENTS

This book is dedicated to my daughter, Avery. I am truly blessed to have you in my life. My mother gave me the gift of faith, and you are my strength and my inspiration. You have been so supportive of me through this trying time. Never in my wildest dreams did I imagine having a daughter as wonderful as you. The love I have for you is beyond comprehension.

INTRODUCTION

A Work in Progress . . .

ALONG WITH THE REST of America, I first heard of *The Real Housewives* in 2006 when Bravo debuted its reality show about the glamorous lives of a group of affluent women in Southern California. Little did I know then that one year later, Bravo would create an equally successful spinoff show set in Manhattan and I would be cast as one of the five original *Real Housewives of New York City*. When we started filming the show I was happily married, I had a successful seven-figure business, and I was the mother of a beautiful twelve-year-old daughter. I never could have anticipated that I was about to enter the most exciting and dramatic chapter of my life. The first episode aired in March of 2008 and, over the course of that first season, Bethenny Frankel, Jill Zarin, LuAnn de Lesepps, Alex McCord and I would embark on a journey that would forever change all of our lives.

Starring in a reality television show is a truly humbling

experience. We open our lives to the scrutiny of the cameras, the media, and millions of viewers who alternately judge, adore, revile, idolize, and ridicule us—sometimes all in the course of one episode. What I never expected when I signed on to do the show, however, was that it would give me the unique opportunity to examine my life from a completely new perspective. Through watching my behavior and my interactions with the other women on the show, I became acutely aware that my past was influencing my present in ways that I am still just beginning to understand. My "unfiltered" personality was shaped by a dysfunctional childhood during which my father verbally and sometimes even physically abused my mother. For most of my life, I kept the truth of my unhappy past a secret. Like many people who have been in abusive situations, I was embarrassed and ashamed. I thought that if I told my friends and colleagues what I had gone through as a child they would judge me, disassociate themselves from me, or think I was inferior to them. Most importantly, I did not want anyone to think of me as a victim . . . because I'm not.

The first time I spoke publicly about my childhood was during the taping of the Season 2 Reunion episode. In response to a viewer question, I revealed for the first time that I grew up in a family where my mother was verbally abused by my father on regular basis. It was liberating to let go of this secret and I decided to open up even more the following season. Over lunch at Fig and Olive, a chic Mediterranean restaurant on the Upper East Side, I told my close friend, Joni, and in turn the 1.75 million viewers who tuned in to watch that episode, what it was like to grow up in a fractured household. My childhood memories were marked by constant fighting, screaming, and crying. For most of my life I hated my father. I hated him for hurting my mother and for making her cry. I hated him for not making me feel loved. I hated him for not providing me with a *normal* childhood. Although I was never physically abused, the events I witnessed in my childhood scarred me emotionally and destroyed my relationship with my father. They also shaped the woman I was to become and tainted my perception of relationships.

After my mother died, my father and I grew even further apart than we already were. Then, three years later, the wildest thing happened. I invited him to spend Christmas with us at our home in Southampton and we actually got along. After a lifetime of resentment, I made peace with him. Then, just two weeks later, he died. Ironically, just when I had finally bonded with my father and he had showed me the love and affection I had been craving my entire life, I lost him for good.

Though the loss was heartbreaking, through his death I was released from the horrible feelings I had been suppressing—the anger, the insecurities, and the shame. Suddenly, a huge burden had been lifted off my shoulders. I will never forget how I felt at that bittersweet moment. It was as if I had finally woken up from a horrible nightmare—the kind where you know you are dreaming but you can't wake yourself up. I had been weighed down and imprisoned by my unresolved emotions towards my father. Now that he was gone I felt reborn, vibrant, and alive. I was *renewed*. It was a powerful awakening. I became introspective and began examining all of the different parts of my life: my relationship with my husband, my career, my sense of faith, my friendships, my self-image, even my lifestyle. I wanted to shout from the rooftop that I was free and open to new experiences and ways to improve myself.

After I shared my story on the show and wrote about it on my blog, I received hundreds of emails. Viewers could not believe that I had kept my secret hidden for so long. They finally understood why I sometimes had such an unedited and unfiltered personality. Many wrote to me wanting to know how they could renew their own lives and what they could do to make peace with their pasts, their parents, their spouses, their friends, their exes, or their body images. At that point in my life, I was on top of the world and I thought I had life all figured out. And then, in 2013, the unthinkable happened; my marriage of over twenty years publicly unraveled.

Having your husband betray you is the worst feeling in the world. I wish it on no one. It made me realize that in life there are no certainties. Every moment is precious and you can't take anything, or anyone, for granted. We are all constantly changing and evolving. We are all works in progress. The important thing is to recognize when you have reached a turning point and to allow yourself to embrace change.

I have learned that renewal is an ongoing journey and, just when you think you have all the answers, life throws you a curveball. Anyone can reinvent themselves at any age. No matter who you are, how old you are, where you come from, or what you have been through, it's never too late to experience true renewal. Very few things in life are ever so bad that you can't wake up, dust yourself off and move toward where you want to be. All it takes is a positive attitude, an open mind to discover the obstacles that are weighing you down, and a willingness to dig deep within yourself and embrace change.

I am opening up about my life, my successes, *and* my failures in this book because I want to share the experiences from which I draw my confidence and determination. No one is perfect . . . especially not me. We all go through ups and downs in life. I've been through a lot. I have earned everything I have and I take nothing for granted. Nothing can hold you back if you don't want it to. When you wake up in the morning, you have a choice; you can either control your fate and work towards renewing certain aspects of your life or you can hide under the covers and complain about your misfortunes. My personal renewal is a journey that is ongoing to this day. I am, and will always be, a work in progress.

My father, Bohdan Mazur

• 1 •

'Twas the Night before Christmas

'TWAS THE NIGHT BEFORE Christmas and all through the house, not a creature was stirring . . . except me. Actually, it was the day before Christmas Eve, 2008, and I was anxiously watching the clock and pacing around the kitchen of the beautiful Southampton home I have shared with my husband, Mario, since our daughter, Avery, was six months old. As I fumbled around a drawer, looking for a bottle opener, I thought about all the holidays we had spent in that house, every Christmas, Thanksgiving, Easter, and birthday for more than a decade. It is a home built on a foundation of love and girded with warm memories of lazy summer days spent by the pool and evenings entertaining friends. It is the home I always dreamt of as a child. It was the home I never had.

This house was my sanctuary—my refuge from the hustle and bustle of city life—but it was about to be penetrated by a potentially hostile force and I was a nervous wreck. For the first time since my mother had passed away from cancer three years earlier, I had invited my father to spend Christmas with us. His health and our relationship had steadily deteriorated since her death and I couldn't even remember the last time we had spoken. I had no idea what kind of mood he would be in. Would he pick on me all week? Would he badger me with below-the-belt jabs? Would there be screaming matches in front of Avery and our other guests? Having located the bottle opener, I poured myself a glass of Pinot Grigio and tried to relax. I closed my eyes and took a long sip. "It's going to be okay," I told myself. But I wasn't convinced.

When the doorbell rang, I nearly jumped out of my skin. I gulped down the last of my wine and placed the empty glass on the marble countertop. As I stood, I looked over at Mario with a smirk and rolled my eyes, as if to say, *this is going to be a disaster and it is all your fault!* A few weeks earlier, he had suggested that I invite my father to spend Christmas with us. "You know, Ramona, your father is getting older. His health is failing. We don't know how much longer he has to live. I think it's important for Avery to spend the holiday with the only grandparent she has left," he reasoned.

My initial reaction was, "You cannot be serious!" I wasn't comfortable with the idea of having my father in my home, especially now that my mother was gone. The last time he visited us in Southampton he drank too much and insulted some friends who had invited us all to dinner in their home. It was such an unpleasant experience that I swore I would never let him in my house again. I had only tolerated being around him in the past for my mother's sake. Now that she had passed away, there was no longer any reason to subject myself to his negative energy and verbal abuse.

"I know you," Mario said, trying to reassure me. "You will regret it if you never get to see him again, never get to talk to him again. Do it for yourself. You need closure. You'll never forgive yourself for not seeing him."

He was speaking from experience. He had made a similar peace with his own father just before he died. Mario's father was an austere German-Italian man who was very stern with his children. Their relationship was always tense, but it became even more strained because they worked together. After I gave birth to Avery, he started to get very sick and it turned out that he had cancer. We would visit him in the hospital and he was so miserable he would say, "Someone

Mario's father, Ernest Singer, visits us in the hospital after Avery is born. He died the day after Avery's christening, but because they had time together Mario was able to find the closure he needed.

just take a gun and shoot me." He deteriorated quickly and Mario became his father's caretaker. He would feed him and help him go to the bathroom. They spent a lot of time together in those final days and bonded. For the first time in his life, his father told Mario that he loved him. He died the day after Avery's christening, but because they had that time together Mario was able to find the closure he needed.

So, there I was, against my better judgment, about to welcome into my home the man I had spent my entire adult life trying to keep at arm's length. My heart was pounding. As I passed our beautifully decorated Christmas tree, I took a deep breath, drawing strength from its familiar piney smell. Half expecting an ogre on the other side, I braced myself and opened the door. No monster; just an old man, looking more frail and diminished than I had ever seen him, accompanied by his grandson (my nephew), Victor, and his mother, Gabriella, who had been serving as his caretaker.

"Hi, daddy," I said timidly, forcing myself to smile. "How are you?"

He looked old, weak, and tired. There was no sparkle in his emerald green eyes. But, even though he was now a sick man in his seventies, when I looked into those eyes I could still see shades of the man who verbally abused my mother my entire life. I shuddered as I recalled a moment that would irrevocably shape the woman I have become . . .

My first birthday.

Me, age four.

I AM FOUR-AND-A-HALF years old.

We live in a quaint Cape Cod-style home in a traditional middle-class suburban town—think Wisteria Lane—far from the Upper East Side. The streets are lined with row after row of houses, with plenty of neighbors and children around. Our backyard, surrounded by a white picket fence, is bursting with an endless variety of colorful flowers.

It is the middle of a sunny afternoon. I am playing with my dolls in the living room when I am jolted by screams coming from the adjacent bedroom. For a moment, I think I must be having a nightmare, but then I see my mother—or at least a woman who looks like my mother—sprinting towards me. Her porcelain white face is covered in crimson blood, her straight brown hair tangled and her brown eyes are wide open, glistening with tears.

"Ramona, call the police!" she screams.

I'm frozen in disbelief. I can't move or speak. Is this really happening? Am I dreaming? I wish it were a nightmare . . . but it isn't. This terrified woman is my mother.

She screams again. "Ramona, call the police!"

I just stare up at her. I drop my doll and run to the square end table. I look at the phone, then at my mom, then at the phone again. I am frightened and confused.

"Mommy, I don't know how to use the telephone," I say, shaking my head. "I don't know how to use it."

A hulking figure appears in the doorway of the living room. I lean forward and stare at him. It is a large, muscular man, with blonde hair, piercing green eyes, and broad shoulders. I rub my eyes, hoping to clear away the terrifying image. He lunges toward my mother. My brown eyes open wider. *That scary man is my daddy!* I think to myself in disbelief. The man who takes me to church every Sunday. The man who passes around the parish's collection basket. The man who takes me to the local bakery to buy cake and cookies. I watch in horror, as he pulls my mother's arm and yanks her out of the living room as if she is one of my lifeless rag dolls. This is the first time I ever saw the monster my father could become when he was drinking.

Sadly, it wasn't the last.

I don't recall my father hitting my mother again until I am eight years old. That's when his aggressive behavior becomes chronic and the abuse escalates to a whole new level.

When I am in second grade, my family moves from our cozy suburban home to a large four-bedroom house in the country. My father, a successful engineer at IBM, is transferred from Poughkeepsie to Kingston, New York. Rather than relocate us to a suburban town like Hyde Park or Rhinebeck, he decides to custom build a house in the isolated, rural town of Staatsburg. Our new home is literally in the middle of the woods; our backyard is overrun with squirrels and rabbits. Our nearest neighbor lives in another isolated house nearly a quarter of a mile away. To the left, seventy-five clear acres separate us from the rest of civilization. There are no neighbors for my mom to talk to; no one to hear her scream and cry while my father abuses her; no one she can run to for help. I think my father planned it this way. We are all alone. We are at his mercy.

The next few years of my life are a blur of nightmarish memories, punctuated by my father drinking too much, then drunkenly abusing and berating my mother. An endless cycle of screaming, fighting, and crying. I feel like I am living in a war zone. One night we are all sitting at the kitchen table eating dinner. My father has just returned from work. He reeks of Scotch. Tonight, as usual, he has stopped at a bar with friends for shots of Scottish whiskey before heading home to terrorize us. Although he would never admit that he has a drinking problem, my father is a functioning alcoholic and a mean drunk. As I shovel buttery potatoes into my mouth, I watch my father slap down his napkin and begin yelling at my mother. I grab my two sisters and brother and run upstairs. My siblings are crying and confused. As the eldest, I feel it is my responsibility to comfort and calm them down. We pile into my tiny bed and hide under the pink quilt, shielding ourselves from the lopsided civil war that is being fought downstairs. But, we can't block out the battle sounds. We hear glasses being broken, ceramic plates shattering against the wall, and my father's strong fist punching the table. Over the loud banging, I hear my mother's small voice pleading, "Stop. Please stop." But my father rages on, drowning her fragile voice out as if she is an inferior servant in his majestic kingdom. In desperation she screams, "If you don't stop, I'll leave you. I'll divorce you."

This actually makes my father— ever the Catholic— pause for a moment. It's the 1960s. No decent Christian woman would ever divorce a handsome, respectable man who fathered her four beautiful children, had a successful job, and put a roof over her head and food on the table. Besides, she has no money. Knowing this, he just mocks her. "Where are you going to go?" He laughs loudly, "You have no money. Who would want you with your four kids?"

Feigning a confidence I know she does not have, my mother screams back, "I don't care. I am getting away from you."

He grabs her by the arm, looks her straight in the eye and says, "If you leave me, I will find you wherever you are. And when I do, I will kill you!"

We are traumatized. Our nerves are shattered. That night, I wet my bed. My sister and brothers do, too. The next day, it happens all over again; my father drinks his Scotch and then berates my mother, while my siblings and I hide under our covers and wet the bed. It happens again, and again, and again. I feel powerless, helpless.

Night after night I fall asleep to the sounds of their fighting. Morning after morning I wake up in a bed of my own urine. Day after day I go to school and pretend that my mother is happy and my father loves us. I am anxious and frightened all the time, but more than that I am ashamed. I can't tell anyone what is going on in our home. I can't invite friends over because I am terrified that they will witness my father's drunken, abusive behavior. I can't sleep at my friends' houses because I worry that I will soil their sheets or my sleeping bag.

Every day I pray, *Please, God. Please make this stop. Please make my father stop picking on my mother.* I ask over and over again, *why is this happening to me? What did I ever do wrong to deserve a life like this?*

But the abuse continues. My father's aggression gets worse and worse until he pushes my mother to the breaking point. One Saturday afternoon, my sisters, brother, and I are playing in the living room downstairs. Once again, we hear my father screaming at my mother. He's yelling at her for spending too much money on groceries. Beneath his stern, booming voice, we hear distressed cries from my mother. "Stop it. You're going to kill me. Stop."

Then, silence.

It is a silence so deafening that I question why I no longer hear my mother crying or my father shouting. Although we usually run and hide when they fight, the initial desperation in her voice and the fear that my father might—or actually did—finally kill my mother compels us to run into the kitchen. There we see our father, his eyes are venomous and he is breathing heavily. He grabs my petite, five-foot-one-inch mother and throws her across the tiled kitchen floor. She is whimpering, begging him to stop. But he doesn't. In a wild rage, he picks her up and flings her defenseless body against the refrigerator. We are crying, jumping up and down, screaming, "Stop, daddy, stop!" But he is oblivious to us. He drags my mother by her long brown hair and thrusts her back and forth. We scream louder, "Daddy, stop! Stop! Stop!" Finally, he looks at us, his eyes coming into focus as if he is coming out of a trance. He storms out of the kitchen, grabs his car keys and drives away.

My mother is hysterical. "We are leaving now. I have to get away from him." She gathers us up and herds us outside. We pile into our wood-paneled station wagon with nothing but the clothes on our backs. "Where are we going?" we ask from the back. She says nothing. She is just shaking uncontrollably, tears streaming down her face. She's swerving all over the road. I have never been so scared. I wonder if I will ever go back home. About thirty minutes later, we are standing in the doorway of her girlfriend Eleanor's house. My mother is begging for a place to stay, somewhere we can hide from my father.

On Sunday, my sisters, brother and I play with Eleanor's four children. Just like other normal kids, we play kickball in the street and monopoly inside the house. We never talk about what happened the night before; we never even acknowledge it. It's as if we have all silently agreed to bury this memory, thinking that if we don't talk about it we can pretend it never really happened. Looking back, it's remarkable what the young mind will do to protect itself from trauma. The next morning, we go to school in Eleanor's children's clothes—underwear and all. That afternoon, my mother picks us up from school and takes us back to our house. She tells us that our father is not coming home. He is never going to hurt her again. I am relieved that he she has stood up for herself and that we don't have to be frightened anymore.

Three months later, my father is back.

Over the next few years, the physical abuse stops but the verbal assaults continue. My mother and father sleep in separate bedrooms, claiming that my father's constant snoring keeps my mom awake at night. But I know better.

I guess the time away sent a message to my father that my mother meant business—that she wouldn't take his *physical* abuse anymore. But that doesn't stop him from *verbally* attacking her . . . or his children. He replaces the punching with nonstop derogatory attacks. And, as time goes on, these assaults worsen. It is as if he is playing a game of chicken with himself, in which he constantly dares to see how aggressive, offensive, and confrontational he can be without becoming physical. Although these attacks leave no bodily scars, they penetrate our psyches and our souls on a much deeper level.

One night he pushes me so far that I snap. I am fifteen. My mother and I are cooking dinner in our large, yellow, eat-in kitchen. I am standing next to the antique stove, preparing the salad, while my mother stands at the opposite counter near the sink. My father walks into the room and demands to know when dinner will be served. My mother tries to placate him, but the more submissive she is the more he bullies her. He's confrontational and belligerent and, as he gains power from his rage, he begins to widen his attack. Suddenly, the abuse isn't only directed toward my mother; it's also directed at me.

My father growls that I am useless and I will never amount to anything. He calls me cruel and demeaning names, some of which I don't fully understand. I try to tune out his voice; the hateful words he utters. But, no matter how hard I try, his badgering is getting to me. He gets in my face. I can smell the rancid alcohol on his breath and see the rancor in his eyes. Then he gets in my mother's face, alternating scathing insults between us. Something he says, I can't recall what, hits a nerve. I snap. My life flashes before my eyes. As if I am rewinding a horror movie, I see images of my mother's battered face begging me to call the police, my father throwing plates, my mother being pulled by her hair, my mother grabbing me so that we can run away from my father, and finally her defeated face as she welcomes him back into our home. I feel so cheated; cheated out of a normal childhood and a loving father. I resent him for exposing me to all this violence and emotional abuse. At that moment, I promise myself that I am not going to be a victim. I am not going to take his abuse. I realize I have to stop him. I have to put him in his place or he will continue to bully me for the rest of my life. I am going to give it right back to him and not back down.

I look over at my mother. She continues to prepare dinner as if there isn't a malicious man berating her in front of her own daughter. I see red. My anger grows like a restless brushfire. Why is she just standing there? Why isn't she fighting back or standing up for herself? I don't get it. How can she stay married to this abusive man? Maybe she's given up, but I haven't. I have to protect her. Sooner or later my father is going to cross that line again and I never want him to hurt her the way he did that night in the kitchen. In that instant, I resolve to stop my father before he takes it too far.

I am aware he is still yelling, but the sound of his voice is just background noise now. Slowly, I open the narrow drawer where my mother keeps the cutlery. I know exactly what I am looking for, the biggest knife with the longest and thickest blade. I pull the largest butcher knife out of the drawer and focus on the sharp blade as it slices through the head of lettuce in front of me. I remind myself, *I am not going to take his shit. I am not going to be a victim anymore.* Then, without hesitation, I lunge toward him, point the sharp blade directly at his face and scream, "Stop it. Stop it right now!" My eyes grow wild. "Stop it right now or I swear I will take this knife and shove it into your neck."

He backs away, startled. But then his mouth twists into a devilish smile and he begins to laugh. This is not the reaction I was expecting. I pull the knife away and take a step back. It all happened so fast. I can't believe what I just did. I don't know who is more shocked—my father, my mother, or *me*. In retrospect, I think my father laughed because he liked that I threatened him. In his warped, sadistic mind he was probably amused by my behavior. Maybe he even respected me a little for standing up to him.

The adrenaline starts to wear off. My body shakes. I am trembling and cannot control myself. My mind is flooded with terrifying questions. *What if he takes his anger at me out on my mother? What would have happened if he had challenged me? Would I have actually stabbed my own father in the neck?* Although he is abusive, I don't want him to die and I certainly didn't want to kill him. I just wanted to send him a message. I wanted him to know what it felt like to be defenseless and afraid. I wanted to threaten and test him the same way he threatened and tested my mother and me. I wanted to watch him back down in fear.

True to form in our family, nothing is said after this incident. No one acknowledges what happened. We don't sit around the dinner table that night and talk about how naughty it was that Ramona pulled a knife on daddy. I'm not sent to a therapist for my anger issues. Instead, we treat it like any other violent episode that occurs in our dysfunctional household; we just sweep it under the carpet and pretend that it never happened. In fact, this is the first time I am sharing this story with anyone.

That day I became my mother's protector and in that moment, I lost forever whatever was left of my childhood. I lost the typical mother-daughter relationship, where the mother protects her daughter. I lost my innocence. But in its place, I gained a sense of empowerment and independence. I became my own advocate, my own protector. On that day, I realized I was on my own.

NOW, HERE I WAS—so many years later— standing in the doorway of my own home staring into the face of the man who had robbed me of my childhood. I shook off the memories and gave him a hug, suppressing my anxiety and turbulent emotions.

This was going to be a long week.

I led my father into the corner guest room, where he was to stay for the next five days because it was on the ground level and he could no longer walk up the stairs. At seventy-four, my father had diabetes and had been suffering from kidney failure. He was visibly weak from the dialysis treatments he was receiving three times a week. Prior to this visit, I had arranged for him to continue these treatments in Southampton with a local doctor. This was no easy task. Try finding a good doctor during the holidays . . . well, try finding one who isn't spending it with his family or vacationing in Aspen or St. Barts. Every decent doctor who hadn't left town for the holiday was fully booked and I had to beg and plead for one to fit my father in—but that's another story.

I asked Avery to take her look-alike cousin, Victor, and his mother to their rooms upstairs. "Bye, Opa," she said excitedly as she left the room. Avery always called my father Opa, which is German for grandpa. I choked up. I'd almost forgotten how much she adored him. Ever since she was a little girl, she wondered why we rarely saw him. She would say, "Mom, I don't understand why you always say your father was such a mean man. I think grandpa's really nice." Of course, I couldn't tell her what he did to my mother—or to me. I only told her, "Avery, you're right. He's very nice to you and I'm glad you have a relationship with him, but he's mellowed over the years. He wasn't that nice to me when I was a kid." I wished I could feel the way she did about his arrival, but there was too much water under the bridge. It was difficult for me to watch her affectionately welcome my father into our home, but how could I begrudge my own daughter the relationship I never had? I understood for the first time that Mario was right. It was important for Avery that I try to set aside my issues with my father—for the moment—and give her this holiday with her last living grandparent. The past few years had been hard on all of us. First we lost Mario's mother and then my own mother three years later.

Both women had been a huge presence in Avery's life. When she was two years old, Mario's mother, Carla, came to live with us. At the age of eighty-one, she had suffered a stroke on the operating table during triple bypass surgery. She lost some of her eyesight, so she could no longer read or play piano, and needed rehab to learn how to hold a fork and knife again. Mario decided she would stay with us for the summer. That visit stretched into months and then years as she began to show signs of dementia. Carla ended up living with us for years and we took care of her. I don't want to say that I didn't have a second child because of her, but having her live with us was as much responsibility as having another child.

When Avery was in kindergarten, Carla developed a clot in her leg. The circulation stopped, gangrene set in, and the doctors told us they had to amputate her leg or she would die. It was such a heart-wrenching decision for Mario to have to make. I remember him saying, "I don't know what to do. If they don't amputate she'll die of gangrene and that's a horrible death, but if they do she's going be so devastated it will kill her anyway." Carla was a beautiful, elegant, vain Italian woman. She dressed in couture, played concert piano, and was a painter and a singer. Mario just kept asking, "How can I tell my mother they have to cut off her leg?" It was so sad.

Because of the stroke and dementia, Carla had already required round-the-clock care, but once she lost her leg we had no choice but to put her into a home. After that, she lost her will to live. She stopped eating. She wouldn't drink anything. When she passed away we had a viewing at Frank Campbell Funeral Chapel on Madison Avenue. We had a closed casket, but at the end of the day, after everyone but us had gone home, Avery looked at Mario and me and said, "I want to see Nanina. I want to say goodbye." We opened up the casket, lifted Avery up and she leaned down to kiss her grandmother goodbye.

After that, I promised Avery things were going to get better, and I really thought they would, but unfortunately, soon after my mother was diagnosed with leukemia. When Avery was little my mother used to come to the city every Monday to take care of her while I was working, so Avery was as close with her as she was with Mario's mother. She was so angry she said to me, "You told me things were going to get better, Mommy. You lied to me." For years we watched my mother fight the cancer, struggling to hang on. But it was a losing battle and she died three years later. On top of losing Mario's mother, it felt like a one-two punch.

Mario set my father's one small bag down in the closet. "Are you hungry?" I asked him, already knowing the answer. "Your granddaughter and I prepared a nice lunch for you. Linguini with fresh clam sauce." My father looked thrilled. He loved good food. I was relieved things seemed to be going smoothly—so far. Despite my misgivings, I intended to do everything in my power to ensure that he had a good time during that visit, even if it meant coordinating outpatient dialysis treatment and spending countless hours in the kitchen.

We walked through our festively decorated living room, which features oversized windows that look out on a majestic pond in the backyard. The smell of fresh pine from the Christmas tree and garland permeated the room. My father didn't say one positive thing about my home or our Christmas decorations. Instead, he headed straight into the large eat-in-kitchen and sat at the head of the country kitchen table—Mario's usual seat—like a king on his throne. This may not seem like a big deal, but the fact that he didn't compliment my home and just plopped down in my husband's seat made my blood boil. His sheer presence made me so feel so anxious and inadequate that everything my father did—or didn't do—became magnified in my mind. On some level, I understood that this was about more than seating arrangements and decorations—this was about him asserting his dominance in *my* home—but in that moment I was too aggravated to think objectively.

I walked past the island countertop and resumed my position at the stove. I stood in front of the Viking free-range, carefully stirring the homemade pasta and aromatic clam sauce. Although my back was to my father, I could feel his green eyes studying me, staring at me. Childhood memories flooded my mind—memories of baking pies, cakes, and cookies in the kitchen in the hopes of receiving his love and approval. My father didn't pay much attention to my sisters or me. He had no interest in our talents and accomplishments. The only time he showed me any love or affection was when I baked him desserts. My mother was a fantastic cook but she wasn't much of a baker. Since we weren't allowed to eat processed box cakes, I became the family's Betty Crocker and I taught myself how to bake from scratch. I would walk down the road to pick apples at the nearby orchard and use them to make homemade apple crisps. Other times, I would make banana bread and cookies. After dinner, my father would eat these treats and I could tell by the sparkle in his eye that he was happy with what I had made, that he was enjoying something that I did. Finally. This was always such a bittersweet moment for me. On one hand, I was overjoyed that my father was acknowledging me—even if it was just for baking—but a huge part of me never understood why he didn't express his appreciation in words or, better yet, with a hug or kiss. Was it too much to ask for some words of recognition or a small compliment? A simple "great job, Ramona" would have made me feel so cherished. All I ever wanted was to feel worthy of his love.

I poured the pasta into a stainless steel colander. As the steam rose up to my face, I closed my eyes and attempted to conjure up a fond memory of my father—but I couldn't. Suddenly, I heard his voice, "Ramona." My heart was pounding. I turned, bracing myself for some kind of dig. "That smells delicious." I was taken aback. A compliment? For more than forty years I had longed for this moment. It may sound strange, but with just those four simple words, I began to relax for the first time all day. My father was actually making an effort to be nice to me. I wondered if he even realized how much those words meant to me. I shrugged my shoulders and thought that *maybe this won't be such a bad week after all.*

I plated the linguini and clam sauce, while Avery sprinkled fresh lemon and parsley over each portion. Mario opened an expensive bottle of Pinot Grigio. I looked at him, telepathically telling him to only pour my father a small glass. I didn't want my father to drink too much. I didn't want any fighting. I didn't want my daughter to see the mean confrontational side of my father. Over the next hour, we ate, drank, and chatted. We behaved as if we were a normal family. There were no plates flying, no fists slamming down on the table, no demeaning insults. So far, so good.

Midway through the meal, my father asked about the menu for Christmas Eve. *Ugh! That's so typical,* I thought to myself. *We haven't even finished eating and he's already thinking about his next meal. Well, at least he isn't yelling at me.*

"So, Ramona, what are we having for dinner tomorrow night?"

Before I could answer, he continued, "Shrimp. It's tradition to have shrimp for Christmas Eve dinner. That's what we're having."

"Okay, dad," I said to appease him. "I'll get shrimp. We'll have shrimp."

"But, not just ordinary shrimp," he smiled mischievously. "It has to be Colossal Shrimp. And you'll need at least two per person."

"Come on, dad. We don't need Colossal Shrimp. Besides, they didn't have them at the fish market when I went to get these clams." I paused and took a deep breath.

I don't think my father, in his seventy-plus years, ever served—let alone ate—Colossal Shrimp in his own home. Money was always a huge source of tension between my parents. My father was a cheap man who constantly berated my mother about money. He would come home and scream at her for spending too much on groceries, never acknowledging that she was shopping for a family of six. I doubt he would have allowed her to indulge on Colossal Shrimp with *his* money. *That's it*, I decided. *I am not going to let him dictate our Christmas Eve dinner. Who is he to come marching into my house demanding that he be served Colossal Shrimp? He'll eat whatever I serve him. He's lucky*

I even invited him! I took a deep breath and exhaled as I tried to clear my head of negativity. I reminded myself that he did seem like he was trying.

"But, I can try another store," I said calmly.

The next day, Avery and I drove to the Clamman, our favorite seafood market in Southampton. As I approached the long glass counter, I scanned the selection of shrimp. I pointed to the extra-large ones and asked the saleswomen for a couple dozen. Immediately, I felt Avery tugging on my arm. She whispered, "Mom, the tag says they're extra-large, not Colossal. Opa wants Colossal Shrimp!"

I decided to humor Avery and asked the saleswomen, "You don't, by any chance, have any Colossal Shrimp?"

"Funny you should ask," she responded. "We're catering a party this evening and happen to have forty extra Colossal Shrimp downstairs."

"Could you bring one up?" I asked.

I had no idea what they even looked like. The woman scurried to the lower level of the store and returned with this huge, ugly, insect-like creature with beady eyes and long pink whiskers. The freakish thing was as big as a lobster—and cost nearly as much!

"Okay, okay. I'll take twelve; butterflied, cleaned, and deveined. Plus, I'll take three quarts of your homemade lobster bisque."

The saleswoman put the slimy, translucent shrimp on the scale. Each one weighed at least 1/3 of a pound, if not more. Despite my aggravation, I did want to please my father. I craved his approval. I always have.

We pulled up in front of our home. Before I could even

put the car in park, Avery grabbed the bag of shrimp and ran to the house, shouting excitedly, "Opa, we got Colossal Shrimp! We got Colossal Shrimp!"

Inside, my father enveloped Avery in a bear hug, "Wait till you have these. You will not believe how delicious they are."

He smiled and I noticed that sparkle in his eye was back. I could see he was happy, but I was hoping for more. I felt empty. I knew I was being foolish, but at that point the shrimp had become more than just freakishly large crustaceans, they represented my father's approval and his respect. I knew it was ridiculous, but a part of me actually believed that if I brought home those shrimp, my father would finally show me he loved me. Ever since I was a little girl watching reruns of *Leave it to Beaver* and *Father Knows Best*, I dreamt of having a father who came home from work in a good mood, asked me about my day, sat at the kitchen table with me while I did my homework, and then tucked me in at night. When I was laying out a small fortune for those Colossal Shrimp, I pictured myself presenting my father with the treasure I had brought home for him. He would be so excited and proud that he would finally compliment me, maybe even give me a hug.

I was wrong. He hugged only my daughter. Once again, he didn't acknowledge me or show me any affection. I tried to remind myself that we were making progress, but I couldn't help wondering *why can't he hug me the way he hugs Avery? What do I have to do for him to show me some love and affection? Am I so naïve as to think that my father can change?*

For the rest of the day, Avery and I prepared Christmas Eve dinner while my father sat at the head of the kitchen table. Mario played jolly Christmas carols throughout the house. We sang along, while we baked butter cookies from scratch. I looked at my father, who had resumed his place at the head of the table. He was smiling at me and humming along to the music.

My favorite thing to do at Christmas is to make cookies with my daughter. It's a Singer family tradition that began when Avery was two years old. As I carefully rolled out the creamy dough on the marble countertop, the smell of sweet cream butter and vanilla extract transported me back in time. I smiled as I recalled my younger self meticulously shaping and cookie-cutting the malleable dough, as Avery happily poured as many red and green sprinkles as she could fit into her tiny, pale hands and then carefully sprinkled them on top of each cookie. The moment they cooled from the oven, she would run to her daddy and give him a cookie. He was the taste-master. And, even if Mario wasn't hungry, he'd devour the cookie and give his little girl a kiss on the cheek, hug her tight, and tell her what a fantastic job she did.

And here we were—years later—still baking these delectable treats. But now, my father had joined us in this family tradition. Avery delicately decorated each cookie with a faint touch as if each buttery confection was a work of art. She handed my father one of her tiny masterpieces for his appraisal. He had become the taste master. He had taken Mario's role—first his seat, then his title. And, he appeared to be enjoying every minute of it. Come to think of it, so was I.

Christmas in Southampton, ca. 2000

"Ramona," he said, "can I have another cookie? They smell great. And they taste even better."

"You know you aren't allowed to eat too many of them. Not with your diabetes."

"Come on, it's Christmas. Besides, my beautiful daughter and granddaughter made them," he said to Avery, with a wink.

I walked over to the table and handed him another cookie. He ate it happily. And, this time, it wasn't Avery who got a hug, it was *me*.

As we finished baking one hundred butter cookies, I felt like my father's arms were still clasped around my waist. Although it may sound strange, this invisible hug lit me up inside and gave me a sense of hope that my father and I might actually get along that week. As I breaded the Colossal Shrimp, I closed my eyes and hoped this feeling would never end.

As the day wore on, I was full of mixed emotions. Although I was ecstatic that my father and I were getting along, there was a part of me that questioned everything he did and wondered why he was never able to be this type of father when I was a little girl. I kept reminding myself to stay positive and enjoy his improved behavior, but there was an uneasy feeling at the back of my mind that I couldn't ignore. I couldn't let go of our history. Sure, I'd gotten a few compliments and even a hug, but that could never make up for all the years I lost.

That evening, as I set the table with my antique gold Minton china for our Christmas Eve dinner, I realized that there were so many things about my father I didn't know.

So much had been left unsaid between us. It's sad that I have so few fond memories of my father. I began to question why he was suddenly behaving differently. Had my mother's death humanized him? Had his dialysis weakened his fighting spirit? Had he finally realized that he was an abusive husband and unloving father? Perhaps he felt the needed to make amends before he died. Or, maybe, he was just happy that I bought him those damn shrimp.

I headed upstairs to my bedroom to change for dinner. As Mario zipped up my gold Michael Kors dress, he tried to calm me, "Quit worrying, Ramona. You and your dad are actually getting along. I haven't heard one below-the-belt jab or condescending comment come out of his mouth in the past two days. Just continue to have an open mind and a positive attitude."

I stared into the mirror and told myself to stop questioning my father's good behavior; to just enjoy it. After all, who knew how long it would last? Suddenly, it dawned on me: *I* am in control of how long it will last. *I* am in control of how my relationship with my father affects me. It's not my father, my husband nor my daughter. Only me. It occurred to me for the first time that, in order to come to peace with myself, I needed to find forgiveness in my heart. I needed to let go of my resentment toward my father and allow myself to release the suppressed feelings of animosity that were holding me back from enjoying this special Christmas Eve . . . from enjoying life. But that was easier said than done.

Before I could explore these thoughts any further, the doorbell rang. It was Mario's best friend, Andrew, and his beautiful girlfriend. Andrew is a warm, handsome man with a down-to-earth, infectious personality. His girlfriend is an elegant woman who looks like a Ralph Lauren model.

We sat at the large, candlelit dining room table. My father sat at one head of the table, while Mario sat at the other. We plated and served creamy lobster bisque while I oversaw the portioning of the Colossal Shrimp. "Two shrimps per plate, please," I said, smiling at my father. Mario opened a nice bottle of white wine and we said grace.

Conversation flowed effortlessly. I do not recall the words that were spoken or the stories that were exchanged, but I do remember the feeling of warmth around the table and the smiles on everyone's faces. My father was polite, even friendly, to my guests, especially Andrew's girlfriend, with whom he was shamelessly flirting. I had to hand it to him; even at the age of seventy-four, he could still admire the grace of a beautiful woman.

I couldn't believe that we were all having such a warm, intimate, engaging dinner. It was a far cry from the last holiday that I had spent with my father five years earlier. At that time, my mother was gravely ill and I wanted her to experience the most special, memorable Christmas. I had bought thousands of dollars worth of Christmas decorations and had even flown in stone crabs from the famous Joe's Stone Crab in Miami. At the last minute, some friends had invited us all over to dinner at their home. We hadn't seen this couple in quite some time so we decided to join them. That was a huge mistake. Throughout the evening, my father repeatedly insulted our hosts. I was mortified. We ended up losing them as friends.

But, I tell myself, *that was then . . . this is now. I need to forgive—though not forget—the past.*

"Ramona," I heard Mario say, "Is everything okay?"

I had fallen into a trance, thinking about Christmas past. Before I answered his question, I glanced over at my father. His green eyes were twinkling like Christmas lights. He was genuinely happy. And that made me happy. For the first time in our lives, I was enjoying his company and he was enjoying mine. It felt like we were a real family. This was the

Me and my father

best Christmas Eve I could remember in years . . . and it seemed like it could only get better.

"Yes, Mario," I smiled. "Everything is perfect."

That night my father, Mario, Avery, and I went to midnight mass at the Basilica of the Sacred Hearts of Jesus and Mary, a beautiful, hundred-year-old Roman Catholic Church in Southampton. I remember my father standing next to me in the pew. We were so close I could feel the warmth of his hand dangling down by his side next to mine. Then, all of a sudden, he grabbed my hand and wove his fingers into mine. I froze in disbelief. This had never happened to me before. I kept very still, barely daring to breath, expecting any moment my father would realize what he had done and drop my hand in disgust. But he continued to clasp my hand in his for the rest of the Mass.

After my initial shock subsided, I felt delighted and exhilarated. The warmth of his hand radiated through my entire body. My heart was so full I felt like it might burst. This was the first time in my life that I had ever held hands with my father. It was like seeing the first snow ever as a child or opening up presents on Christmas morning. It was the most fantastic feeling in the whole world. Santa Claus had come early for me that year.

When it was time for my father to go home, I remember saying goodbye to him at the door and, for the first time in my life, feeling sad to see him leave. Finally, we had connected. I was enjoying his company so much that I wasn't ready for our time together to end.

"Dad, please, can't you stay? Do you really need to go so soon? I really want you to stay a little longer," I said.

I got very emotional and I started to cry.

"No," he insisted, "I can't stay. I need to get home. I have my dialysis. I have things to do. We'll see each other again soon."

He died two weeks later. I never got to see my father again. We had finally turned a corner in our relationship, and now he was gone forever.

By opening up about my childhood, I have learned that there are many people like me who have been crippled by their past. Maybe my father did the best he could, maybe not. Either way, my childhood was awful and the memory of it still haunts me to this day. I will never excuse my father's behavior. But, for my own sake, for my own happiness, I needed to forgive him. That doesn't mean I will forget the past, but I realized that the hatred and resentment I had been holding onto was self-destructive. I finally understood that I needed to move on. I learned the importance of forgiveness, for my own well-being. I needed to come to terms with my past, what my father did to my mother, and my relationship with him. I needed to do this for myself.

Through my father's death, I was released from the negativity that had clouded all of my childhood memories. The toxicity surrounding my life slowly faded away. In its place I found a sense of peace and forgiveness. I emerged from hell and was brought into the light.

My mother, Veronika Mazur

• 2 •

Always Let Faith Be Your Guide

I AM SITTING IN THE living room of my childhood home, staring out the big picture window that faces our front yard and looks out at the majestic Hudson River in the distance. I am fourteen-years-old. It is spring and the dogwood is beginning to bloom. But I am looking beyond the sea of white blossoms glistening in the sunlight. I am daydreaming again; I'm imagining a life beyond this window. One filled with love, happiness, and success. A life in which I have a father who comes home from work, hands some flowers to my mother, and then gives us each a kiss us on the cheek. A life where we sit around the dinner table and talk about our day.

I am so lost in this alternate reality that I barely notice my mother appear beside me. She stands with her back to the window and faces me. She has a look that I have never seen before. She starts to speak and I can tell by her solemn tone that she has something difficult to say. I just listen.

"Ramona, I want you to know that I pray to God every

night that you don't make the same mistakes that I made. I pray to God that you will have a better life than mine."

It's as if my mother has read my mind. Could she know that I was sitting at this window dreaming of a different life, one better than hers?

"What do you mean?" I ask timidly.

"I don't want you to end up like me. I was so young when I met your father. I was a senior in high school, not much older than you are now. I was instantly attracted to your father. He was so handsome and he seemed like such an adult to me; he already had a great job and earned a nice living. We fell in love. I was supposed to attend Vassar College in the fall. I wanted to get a degree and have a career." She pauses, and I can tell she is struggling to find the words for what she has to say next, "But then the unthinkable happened. I got pregnant—with *you*. I knew I couldn't give you up."

I take a deep breath. I say nothing. I am speechless. I can't believe what my mother is telling me. I never knew that I was an unplanned pregnancy, that *I* was the reason my mother married my father. I never knew that my mother had wanted to go to college and that she had to give up that dream because of me. I am overwhelmed with guilt. I wonder if she blames me for her unhappy life.

YEARS LATER, WHEN my mother was in the hospital dying, I realized that even though she married my father because she got pregnant, the real reason she stayed with him was because he had given her the home she never had as a child. My mother was a Hungarian refugee who came to this country when she was fourteen or fifteen years old. She was born in Budapest and at some point during the 1940s, she and her mother were forced to leave their homeland and flee to Austria. I don't know much about how or why she fled—she didn't like to talk about it—but my understanding is that Budapest was being bombed and they had to leave or they would die. They ended up in a displaced persons camp in Austria because the only way to get into the United States at that point was through one of these camps.

My grandmother didn't speak German so my mother became her interpreter, her connection to the world. She was barely in her teens, but she took on this adult role of negotiating everything from haggling for food to dealing with the paperwork they needed to get into the United States. I'm not sure how long they lived like this—maybe six months, maybe a year, maybe two—but eventually a Hungarian church in Poughkeepsie sponsored them to come to America. With little more than the clothes on their backs, they left Austria and settled in the Hudson Valley in upstate New York. To support them in this new life, my grandmother took different jobs working for people in their homes as a cook. They moved from house to house, never settling anywhere long enough for my mother to set down roots. I can't imagine how horrible it must have been for her to lose her home and end up living in a DP camp, only to come to the United States and still not really have a home. She was so young that this chaotic life and lack of stability must have had a huge impact on her.

A few years after they arrived in the States, she met my father at a Polish polka dance. He had graduated from engineering school and had a good job at IBM. My mother was a very beautiful, intelligent woman, but once she got pregnant it must have seemed that marrying my father was the best option she had to make a good life for herself. My father built her a big house in the country and I know this house was deeply important to her. I believe a big part of the reason she never left him was that she didn't want to leave the only real home she ever had. At that time there were no shelters for battered women, no resources for women like her. My father would say, "Where are you going to go? You have four kids. If you leave me, you'll have no money, no home." Nothing frightened my mother more than the idea of becoming displaced again.

My father was the youngest of six children. He grew up during the depression in the Hill District of Pittsburgh. His parents were Ukrainian immigrants who met on the boat coming to the United States. His father was a carpenter and his mother was a stern, sadistic woman who was physically and verbally abusive. The oldest three of his siblings were girls and they actually wanted to take him away from their mother because she was so abusive. I remember my aunt Stella, who was twelve years older than my father, telling me stories of how their mother would make him soak in a warm bath before she would beat him so that his skin would soften and it would hurt more. It's not surprising he became a misogynist and grew up to perpetuate the cycle of abuse. The only fond memories I have of my father during my childhood are the times he played games with us. When he wasn't drinking, he could actually be very charming and creative. He used to make up all kinds of games for us to play. There was "Button, Button" where we'd all line up with our hands out, palms together. He'd pass his own closed hands over each of ours, drop a button into one of our hands and say, "Button, button, who has the button?" We also used to play a game

Mazur family portrait: me, my mother and father, and my siblings (Tanya, Sonya, and Nick)

he made up called "Tin Can Alley," where he'd line up his beer cans for us to kick into a makeshift goal. Whoever got closest won the game. My mother was a great homemaker, but my father was the creative one.

As I got older, he and I would butt heads because I was the eldest and I was very strong-willed and independent. I definitely inherited some of his antagonistic streak; when I feel that I'm being attacked, I can sometimes go below the belt say hurtful things without thinking. I decided when I was fifteen-years-old that I wasn't going to take his crap anymore, or anyone else's for that matter. My mother was very non-confrontational and, after I stood up to my father in the kitchen that day, I became her defender. After that, he became less aggressive with me, but he withheld his love and approval—which is another kind of abuse. He basically ignored me, and when he wasn't ignoring me he was criticizing me.

My mother did try to leave him a couple of times, but she always came back. When things got really bad, she'd take us to Brooklyn, where my grandmother lived, to get away from him for a few days. One time when I was six or seven, we stayed there for a week. My grandmother lived in a tiny, one-bedroom apartment and we had to sleep on the living room floor. It was awful. I just wanted to go home, to sleep in my own bed in my own bedroom. We weren't really allowed to go out, so most of the time we were just cooped up in this tiny apartment. The only time I remember leaving the apartment was when my mom took us on the subway to visit the World's Fair.

At night, my father would call and I could hear my grandmother saying, "No, Veronika's not here. I don't

know where she is." I remember thinking, *why is my grandmother not telling my father where we are?* I was old enough to know something wasn't right, but not old enough to understand what was going on. Maybe I didn't want to know.

EVEN THOUGH I can tell sharing these memories with me is painful, my mother steels herself and continues, "After I found out I was pregnant, your father decided the respectable thing to do was to get married. So we did. And then we had you, and later your brother and your sisters. So I never went to college." This is the first time my mother has ever acknowledged to me, or anyone, that she has felt trapped in an unhappy marriage. No matter how much my father drinks or how mean he gets when he does, we have always known never to speak about it with my mother.

My mother and father on their wedding day, ca. 1956

My heart breaks for my mother. She keeps reassuring me how happy she has been with her four children and that we are the only source of joy in her life. But I know that beneath it all she is profoundly sad about how her life turned out. She talks for a long time. She is so honest, so vulnerable. It's hard for me to take it all in. I keep wondering how she has been able to hold it together all these years. Where does she find the strength to wake up every day and go on living given what she has endured?

"But, Mom," I say crying. "Why do you stay with Daddy? Can't you just leave him?"

"I have no choice. I have no education, no money of my own. How would I support four children on my own? It's impossible."

"What about a divorce? Couldn't you get child support?" I'm not even sure I know what this means, but I ask anyway.

"It's not that simple, Ramona. Your father said if I ever divorced him, he'd quit his job at IBM and then we would have no money. And I have no way to earn enough money to support four children. And even if I could get a divorce, you've heard your father. He swore that if I left him, he would find me and kill me. I can't have my children be without a mother." Her voice cracks, "I can't."

She takes a deep breath and continues, "Ramona, I pray to God every night that you go to college. I pray that you get an education, so you can have a career and never have to depend on a man. I pray you that you will be able to support yourself so you can marry for love, not for money or stability. I pray for you to become a strong independent woman, so you will never feel trapped like me."

"Okay, Mom," I say, trying to calm her down. "I promise. I will go to college and make money and have my own career." As the words come out of my mouth, I am not even sure what it is that I am saying. I am fourteen-years-old and it's the 1970s, for God's sake. All I know is that I am making a promise to my mother and I am going to keep it. After all, I do want a better life and if going to college and making money is what is going to grant me my wish, then that is exactly what I am going to do.

Finally, my mother gives in to the tears she has been fighting back, "And, no matter what, you must keep your faith. You must always ask for God's help, mercy, and forgiveness. You must have faith in God, Ramona, and you must have faith in yourself. Always know that if you have faith, *true faith*, you can accomplish anything."

Finally, I understand. My mother is able to endure her life because she has faith, faith that her children's lives will be better than hers.

For the next three years, I sit at that window every day. I stare out into the distance and think about my mother's advice. I will have true faith. I no longer just daydream of a better life; I have faith it will happen. I will make it happen. I ask God to help me, "Please God, I know there is a better life out there for me. Please God, save me from this life. Please God, give me the strength I need to build a better life for myself. Please, God, help me find a better life. Please. Please. *Please*."

When my mother was diagnosed with leukemia in 2003, she was given only three months to live. It was a huge blow for all of us, but especially for my father. As he got older my father had softened and, by the time they were in their fifties, he and my mother had actually settled into a nice relationship. Maybe it was the stress that raising four kids put on them, but once all of us were out of the house my father stopped drinking as much. He became less aggressive and he and my mother actually got along fairly well. They really did love each other, but they had a very volatile relationship. He could still be very antagonistic at times and go for the verbal jugular, but I guess my mother learned not to let it bother her.

After she was diagnosed, my mother went through chemotherapy and began doing protocol experimental treatments at Sloan-Kettering. She deteriorated quickly and within a few months she weighed only ninety-five pounds

My mother and father with Avery, 1996

and was bedridden. I would cook for her every day and bring her special food in the hospital, but within a week she was so weak she couldn't even pick her head up from the pillow. I was devastated. I remember Mario saying to me, "Ramona, face it. Your mother's going to die. You just have to accept it."

I looked at him and I said, "My mother is not dying in this hospital. If she's going to die anywhere she's going to die at home. I am not going to allow this to happen."

I could see how hard my mom was struggling to hang on and I decided I wasn't going to let her go without a fight. I looked at her chart, wrote down every medication she was on, and went to my local pharmacy. I showed them the list and they said they couldn't understand why she was on one of the medications because it was so powerful it would lay out a two-hundred-pound man. I told my father what I had learned, but he didn't have the courage to do anything about it. So I went back to the hospital and told the doctors myself that they had to take my mother off that medication. I remember them saying she would die if they did, but I told them, "This medicine is killing her anyway. Take her off it now." They agreed to wean her off it gradually. Four days later my mother was smiling and sitting up in bed, looking perky and happy.

It took six months for her just to recover from the chemo and that medication. When she was strong enough, I found a doctor who worked with alternative medicines. Using coenzymes and shark cartilage treatments, he restored her to near perfect health. For a full year, she was almost like her old self, but then she got sick again. Eventually, she was admitted to her local hospital in Kingston, New York, and we were told there was nothing more they could for her. My father wanted to put her into hospice, but I remember my mother crying, "I don't want to die. I'm not ready to die. Please help me, Ramona." I contacted the head oncologist at New York Presbyterian Hospital and told him about my mom.

I said, "All I want is for my mother to have a good quality of life. Can you extend her life so that she has that?"

He told me, "Yes, I think we can do that."

My father was upset that I was stepping in. It was hard for him to deal with the fact that my mother was sick and dying. We all knew, especially my mother, that he wouldn't last long without her. I said to him, "You know what, Dad? If you were sick and you needed help, wouldn't you want me to help you? How can you not let me help Mom?"

Finally, he relented and they transported my mother by ambulance to New York Presbyterian Hospital in the city. She had another good month, but then she was in and out of hospitals for the next year until she was so sick my father was too afraid take her home. She refused to go into hospice, so her doctor agreed to keep her in the hospital as long as possible.

I sat by her side for days, watching her get weaker and weaker. For the first time since that conversation we had when I was fourteen, my mother and I spoke about her life before she met my father. I knew she and her mother were refugees, but I learned that even after they got to this country she still had very little stability because my grandmother moved them around so much. One afternoon in the hospital, as I held her hand and tried to encourage her to eat, my mother said to me, "Once, my mother worked as a cook for a woman who lived in a big, beautiful house in the country. I loved that house. I wanted to stay there, but my mother was lonely and decided to move us to Poughkeepsie to find work closer to the Hungarian church. I was so sad to leave, Ramona. I really loved that house."

By this point, my mother was deteriorating so rapidly her doctor decided it was finally time to move her into hospice. She died at four o'clock the following morning. It was New Year's Day. Earlier that evening I had been with my family celebrating New Year's Eve and we didn't get home until late. I was in a very deep sleep and I suddenly jolted awake, which is very unusual for me. My mother's image came to me and I knew in that moment that she was gone. I looked at the clock and it was 4:00 a.m. My father died three years and two weeks later. Those last three years we had with my mother were a miracle. She was a fighter. She never gave up. I get my strength and resilience from her; it is the greatest gift a mother can give to her children.

To this day, I still believe she should have left my father. As much as I love and admire my mother, I can't understand her decision to stay with an abusive husband. Even though things got better between them as they got older, what my siblings and I witnessed as children left us emotionally scarred and altered our perception of relationships and marriage. But, I don't blame my mother. I understand now that she was too afraid to leave. Not only because she was worried about supporting us, but also because she was too broken to walk away from the only real home she ever had. To her, our house represented the stability she never had as a young girl.

As soon as I turned seventeen and graduated from high school, I left home and never looked back. I moved to New York City to study fashion and earned a B.S. Degree in Business from FIT. I started out as a buyer for Macy's, created my own successful fashion business by the age of twenty-nine, married for love, and had a beautiful daughter in my thirties. I had everything my mother ever dreamed I would have.

Once I moved out, I never wanted to go back home because I couldn't stand to be around my father. Sometimes, in an effort to entice me to come home, my mother would call me up and say, "Ramona, the dogwood is blooming. You love when it blooms. Come home so you can see it." Because we lived in the woods, the only type of blooms that would flower in the spring were the beautiful white blossoms of the dogwood trees. It grows so thick it looks like snow between the trees. I can still close my eyes and see it through the big picture window in the living room, where I sat for years patiently praying for a better life.

Looking back, I still cannot believe that my mother told me I was an unplanned baby when I was just fourteen-years-old. I am glad she did, though, because it brought us closer together. It was the longest one-on-one conversation I would have with my mother until just before she died. It was the first time she spoke openly about her relationship with my father—how they met, why they got married, and why she put up with his abuse. Prior to this conversation, my father's behavior was always a massive elephant in the room that we pretended didn't exist. She must have felt so trapped, so alone, so scared. In her mind, she only had one option; she had to stay in her marriage forever and just pray that the lives of her children would be better than hers.

As a mother of a twenty-year-old daughter, I can only imagine the courage it took for my mother to confide in me that she had failed to realize her dreams. Although she was a petite woman who was bullied by my father on a daily basis, she was—and always will be—my hero, my inspiration, and my source of strength. That day, she taught me an important lesson that has become a defining principle in my life. I will always have true faith.

Me, age 15

· 3 ·

Fashion Forward

I HAVE ALWAYS BEEN VERY goal-oriented. At ten years old I didn't necessarily know what I wanted to be when I grew up, but I knew that I needed to get straight As. I loved math and analyzing numbers. By the age of fifteen I knew I wanted to combine business with fashion. Initially, I considered getting my bachelor's degree in business, but after I spent the summer in New York City as an assistant buyer, I knew fashion was the only road for me. The Fashion Institute of Technology had just opened its first four-year program. It was a very exclusive honors program. Three months before the start of its inaugural semester, I went to see the dean and convinced him to admit me. Sometimes, in life and in business, you just have to go for it.

I have always taken professional risks, always thought three steps ahead when it comes to my career. Even before I got into FIT, I had a plan for my future. *One step ahead*: I wanted to study business and fashion. *Two steps ahead*: I wanted to get into a buying training program. *Three steps*

Me, age 27, ca. 1983

ahead: I wanted to become a buyer for a top department store. So I called the person who hired part-time executive help for Macy's. Because I had the courage to go for it, I got a job as a part-time sales manager, which paved the way for me to get into a top buying program and, ultimately, to becoming a buyer for Macy's. I started out as a sales girl on the floor and worked my way up to Acting Sales Manager. I wound up taking twenty-one credits and working a thirty-five-hour week, but it was worth it because I was on my way to realizing my dream of working in fashion.

In my twenties I was full of energy and ambition and I was determined to make my mark in fashion as a business-woman. In the 80s I worked for Calvin Klein, when Brooke Shields was doing the now legendary advertising campaign for the newly launched CK Calvin Klein Jeans label, and from there I went to French Connection. I wanted to get out of the junior market and into missy, which was adult sizes, so I started working for Flora Kung, a fashion designer who was known for her vibrant silk dresses and free-hand prints. I was managing a new division for her and traveling all over the country, opening accounts with upscale department stores like Neiman Marcus, Bergdorfs, and Marshall Field's. From there I went to work for a company called Cygne Designs that did private production for stores like The Limited, Express, Anne Taylor, and Talbots. The founder, Irving Benson, was married to a woman by the name of Diane B, who had a beautiful high-end collection. She had her own boutiques, but she also sold to specialty stores and department stores and I was brought on as a sales manager for her line. Right away, I was booking as much as the two girls that were already working there, so I was bringing in fifty percent of the business. I was good at sales because I loved working in fashion and I was very aggressive.

Eventually, Mast Holdings, a subsidiary of The Limited, came in and acquired eighty percent of Cygne Designs. I was told they would keep me on to run the fashion line, but just before the company went public Mast decided to shut down Diane B. My boss came to me and said, "We want to keep you on. We're just waiting to get some refinancing for the Diane B line. In the meantime, we have excess inventory that we need to get rid of. Do you think you can help us out?" Now, this was something I had not done before. I had been selling high-end fashions to department stores and they were asking me to liquidate millions of units of overstock—quickly. But I approached the challenge like any other in my life; I embraced it with a positive attitude.

In the end, I exceeded everyone's expectations, even my own. I sold millions of dollars worth of inventory in just a couple of weeks. My bosses were shocked, but for me it was simple. I understood that everything in business is about playing the game and getting the order. If I had a pant or a top that I knew I only needed to sell for eight dollars a unit, I would ask for ten. *Rule #1: Always start high*. If they offered me seven dollars, I would say, "Okay, I can take your order for seven dollars. I'll hold it to the side, but I can't promise you'll get shipped. If get a better offer, I'll have to take it . . . but if we write the order up right now for eight dollars, I will guarantee that you will get shipped." It almost always worked and I would end up writing the order for eight dollars. *Rule #2: Know what you're selling and stick to your guns.*

After six months, Cygne couldn't find financing for the Diane B line so the firm closed it down and I was laid off. Meanwhile, I had been dating a doctor for a few years. We were engaged to be married, but he had commitment issues and I could never get him to set the date. I had tried to break up with him several times, but he always found a way to reel me back in. Then one day I realized that I always knew I would never end up marrying him. Subconsciously, I had intentionally picked the wrong guy. Yes, on paper, he looked good. He was a doctor. He was successful, funny, handsome, and smart, but he was emotionally distant—like my father. Finally, I realized that I was better off without him.

I remember, one day I decided I'd had enough and I just packed up all my things. I hadn't officially moved in with him, but I hardly ever stayed at my own place anymore. I had kept my own apartment because somehow I must have known not to give it up. I couldn't stand my roommate at the time, but now I was relieved I hadn't moved out. I hired some guys from the Food Emporium down the block to help me with my boxes, borrowed my ex's Jaguar from his garage, loaded it up with my stuff, and drove it to my old apartment. When he got home that night, there was no trace that I was ever there, not even a Tampax or a jar of nail polish. Nothing.

They say the three things in life you need the most are love, home, and career. I was moving back in with a roommate I couldn't stand—*strike one*. I had just left the man I thought I was going to marry—*strike two*. And I had been laid off from my job—*strike three!* Suddenly, everything I had been working for seemed to be falling apart, but I made a very conscious decision that I would not stop believing in myself. I've always been very frugal, I have always saved my money, and I never ever spend over my means. But I decided to do something very frivolous. I took the $5,000 severance I got from Cygne and bought myself the most magnificent Golden Isle fox fur coat that I had ever seen. It complemented my long blonde hair perfectly and I felt so fabulous and glamorous in it. I had worked hard my entire life, supported myself through college, and watched every penny I made, but I made a very deliberate decision to use that money to take care of *me*, to make an investment in myself. So here I was, pushing thirty, no fiancé and no job, even my living situation was unstable . . . but I had a *fabulous* fur coat. I knew that I had to take back control of my life. I began looking for a new apartment, I resolved to start dating again, and started working to get my career back on track.

As fate would have it, on the day I moved back into my apartment the phone rang and it was Mario. We had gone out on one date a few years back, but we kept getting our wires crossed and never hooked up for a second date. I often saw him around the gym and we flirted shamelessly, but we were both involved with other people so it never went anywhere. Then, out of the blue, he called me up and said, "I want you to know, I just ended it with the girl I was dating and I was curious if you're still in a relationship."

I said, "Well, funny you should ask. You're going to be the first to know that I just ended my engagement."

"Great," he said. "Let's have dinner."

"Didn't you hear what I said? I just broke off the engagement with the man I was planning to marry. I don't want to go out on a date."

But Mario was persistent and charming, and I ended up agreeing to go out with him. I didn't want it to feel too much like a date so I arranged to meet him at the restaurant. I remember walking in and spotting him sitting at the table. He stood up and when our eyes met, it was like thunderbolts. We had an instant, intense connection. It was unlike anything I had ever experienced before. We started dating, but after ten months I realized something was holding me back. I was terrified of marriage and I knew Mario wanted a wife and a family. I didn't want to hurt him, so we broke up. It was painful. I remember both of us crying and him saying, "I love you and I know you love me." I did love him, very much, but I knew I wasn't being fair to him. I knew he wanted to marry me, but I just couldn't turn the corner. I wasn't ready. I was afraid to commit to marriage because it felt claustrophobic to me. I was afraid of getting close to someone because my mother had such a bad relationship with my father. Before Mario, I had chosen to be with men who were charming and good looking but who were emotionally distant and cold—like my father. I wanted to have to win their attention and affection, but it was safe because I knew I never would. I was afraid to really care about someone and be vulnerable. I realized I needed to work on myself before I could be in a healthy relationship. I started seeing a therapist three times a week and eventually she helped me to see that marriage is a partnership, not a prison. Once I learned that, I was able to take a leap of faith. After six months, Mario and I got back together again and within a few months we were engaged.

Meanwhile, the accountant from Cygne Designs had called me up and said, "Ramona, we still have excess inventory and I don't have time to get rid it. Why don't you buy it from us and resell it yourself?" They only wanted $100,000 for it and I knew I could sell it and easily make a twenty percent profit for myself. The only problem was coming up with the initial money to buy the stock. So I picked up the phone and started hustling. I got $25,000 in prepaid orders, but I still had another $75,000 I needed to come up with.

I knew this well-to-do businessman, who had been a

mentor to me, and he offered to put up the remaining cash, but I would have to make him a partner and give him a percentage of the business. I decided to call up my father and ask for his advice. When I heard his voice on the other end of the phone, I could already hear the judgment in his voice, but I took a deep breath and dove right in, "Hi, Dad. I need to ask your advice. I've been selling closeouts for Cygne, but now I have a chance to do it on my own. It's an amazing business opportunity for me. There's no risk because I only take the order if I have the merchandise presold and all the accounts I sell to have AAA credit ratings. I need to pre-pay for the merchandise and there's a businessman who wants to partner with me. He's offered to put up the cash I need and he—"

My father cut me off and I will never forget what he said next. "Ramona, in business you need no partners. How much do you need?"

"Seventy-five thousand."

Without hesitation he said, "Okay, I'll write the check and send it to you today."

I almost peed in my pants. This is was a man who probably saved eighty cents of every dollar he ever made. He was a penny pincher. Every week, without fail, he gave my mother a hard time no matter how much—or how little—she spent on groceries. To my father, $75,000 was the equivalent of a million bucks, but he didn't miss a beat when I told him how much I needed. My father, Mr. Miser, who didn't like women, who didn't believe I would ever amount to anything, was cutting me a check for seventy-five grand? I couldn't believe it.

I paid him back in thirty days, plus interest. I was a little pissed off that he made me pay the interest, but I was still grateful that he lent me the money. After that, my mother would tell me how he would brag about his daughter to all his friends. He didn't quite tell me to my face, but for the first time in my life I knew he was proud of me. It was a big moment in our relationship. As bad as he was all those years when I was growing up, for him to step up and help me like that was the last thing I ever expected from him. After that, our relationship didn't exactly improve, but I actually willingly went home that Christmas. And that was huge for me. I hadn't been home for Christmas in at least ten years.

That's how I became a jobber and started my first business, RMS Fashions, Inc. I bought and sold excess inventory and I ended up making a lot of money doing it. When I started out I had no idea I would be in the business for the next twenty years. At first, I was just working out of a large handbag, but I quickly decided to get my own office and commit to a one-year lease for $12,000. I figured, *if I don't make a penny this year, what's the worst that can happen? I'll be out twelve grand. Okay, I'll take that risk*. I went out in the market not knowing who to buy from, but I'd look up manufacturers' names and cold call. I'd walk into a showroom, find out who was in charge of selling excess inventory and introduce myself. Then I'd follow up and call them again. I was aggressive and ambitious. If I heard Express had canceled 50,000 units of a top, I would buy the lot from them and send it to my own warehouse. To eliminate risk, I'd always have preorders in place with stores like

TJ Maxx, Marshalls, Ross Stores, and Burlington Coat Factory. I was always scanning for opportunities. If I read an article in *Women's Wear* about some designer closing its dress division, I'd call the company and ask about its inventory. I'd usually walk out with a purchase order for 50,000 dresses that I, of course, had already presold to my buyers. My customers loved me and they knew that I always shipped a quality product, but tracking down inventory wasn't always easy. My biggest challenge was that I was always having to reinvent myself because I couldn't buy the same product from the same manufacturer all the time. They were selling to me at a loss and if they sold to me all the time they'd go out of business. So I was constantly on the hunt, like a squirrel looking for a nut.

I was successful right out of the gate because I knew how to control my cash flow and that's what can make or break a business. My first order was from a customer who I had known for a couple of years, so I was able to ask the company to prepay me. I actually remember getting that first check for $50,000. I just kept thinking, *holy shit. Fifty grand. Made out to me.* After that, I would make sure the stores paid me in ten days. Most stores pay you net sixty days, but my customers wanted my product and I was persistent enough that I demanded ten days and got it. I would get thirty-day terms from the manufacturers and, with ten-day terms from my buyer, I always had a float of twenty days of money. These are typically unheard of terms in any business. I actually had the opposite problem from most businesses. I had excess cash in my account at all times. This was such an exciting period of my life because I was working fewer hours, making more money, and—best of all—I was making it all for myself.

I worked hard and saved my money. As a result, I had seven figures in the bank before I was even married. Funnily enough, I had my most financially successful year when I was pregnant with Avery. That year, I made three deals in a row for a quarter of a million dollars each. Profit. Usually my deals were for $10,000 profit or $20,000 profit. I believe God was looking out for me. I was in my late thirties, running my own business, and about to have a baby. I had no idea if I was going to be able to keep working the way I had been. With those three deals, I had enough money that, no matter what happened with the pregnancy or the new baby, I could take a year off from work if necessary.

God was truly looking out for me that year. Not only was my business stronger than ever, when Avery was four months old, we found our beautiful house in the Hamptons. I had been looking at real estate out there even before Mario and I were engaged. I have always believed in real estate. Everyone else I knew was investing in the stock market, but I came from a middle class family, I worked hard for my money, and I just didn't trust the market. I knew I wanted to buy a home with my savings and I was confident that I had a good eye for real estate. The moment I saw the house, which at the time was selling for $875,000, I fell in love and used my premarital savings to buy it. I put my heart and soul into that house. We closed in November and, over the next six months, I invested $500,000 and completely redecorated all 7,000 square feet of the house, complete with curtains, furnishings, and landscaping. We celebrated

Holding Avery in the hospital, just after her birth

Avery, age 4, perched on the bathroom Jacuzzi

Avery's first birthday there the following May. This would be the first of many happy family memories in that house. I realized when my mother was on her deathbed that we both projected our sense of stability onto our homes. I must have picked that up from her without even understanding that she had felt that way until just before she died.

In many ways, for me the house in Southampton was also a "fuck you" to my father. I will never forget when I was in college how he'd complain, "Why should I pay for your last two years? You're just going to get married and have kids." He didn't believe in me, not until I was well into my twenties and already had a successful career. Although it meant a lot to me that he supported me when I started my own business, it wasn't until I bought that house that I felt that I had truly proved myself. It's not only my home; it's a badge of my success. Even though I bought it after Mario and I were married, he would always refer to it as "your house" or "her house." That house became such a deep part of me. I needed it for my own identity. It was the home I never had. It represented love and became a part of my soul.

However, without my realizing it, this need for independence was slowly eroding my marriage. In the beginning, Mario wasn't threatened by my success. He was proud to have such an ambitious, strong woman by his side. It was those qualities that drew him to me in the first place. But, as his own business began to struggle, my success and need for independence began slowly, but steadily, pushing us apart.

Enter, *The Real Housewives of New York City* . . .

It is the middle of the summer of 2007, the days are long and hot and business is very slow. I am working with one of my manufacturers when my cell phone rings. It's my friend, Dr. Sharon Giese, a prominent plastic surgeon and expert on natural anti-aging procedures. She says, "I was approached by a producer from Bravo. They're doing some kind of a reality television show about women in New York City who are married, live an upscale lifestyle, and are very social. Right away, I thought of you. Would you be interested?"

I'm bored, it's the end of July, the deadest time of the year in my line work, so I say, "What the heck? I'll do it just for the hell of it. Give them my number."

A few weeks later, a small camera crew comes out for the day. They film me at my office, going to appointments, at home, and with Avery, who is twelve years old. She is very excited about this opportunity to be on television. She has been interested in acting, but we never pursued it for her because it's such a demanding business and school has always come first.

Avery and I decide to go shopping at Lester's, one of our favorite stores. The cameras follow us around the store but I hardly notice them. I just go about my day as usual. I'm sorting through a rack of clothing when Avery tugs on my arm and whispers, "Mommy, everyone's looking at us. They're staring at us!" I roll my eyes and say, "Oh, Ave, just pretend the cameras aren't there." It's easy for me to block out the cameras, probably because growing up I had to block out all the noise in my family. I shut the cameras out, just like I shut out my father's yelling.

We spend the entire day filming and it's exhausting but fun. At one point Avery says to me, "Oh, my God. This is so much work, Mommy." I had been filming all day long and she only filmed for two hours with me. I say to her, "Avery, if you want to be an actor, this is what it's about. We're just doing a demo tape for a reality show here. It would be ten times more work if you were filming a movie."

When we get back to our apartment, Avery is excited. She keeps asking, "Are we gonna be on, Mommy? Do you think we'll be on the show? Is this it? Is this it?" But the producer explains that the six hours of footage have to be edited down to a two-minute video that she will submit to the head producers of the show. They are the ones who will make the final decision. She tells us, "I'll get back to you."

The funny thing is, when she does get back to me it turns out the head producer has already seen me on another woman's demo tape. I had almost forgotten, but a few months back I had attended a cooking party, hosted by my friend Pamela Morgan, who owns a culinary business called Flirting with Flavors. During the party, I was my usual animated, outgoing, gregarious self, bopping around and asking questions. When the head producer watched the tape and saw me, she asked, "Who is that woman? Let's find *her*." Apparently, they tried to track me down, but they couldn't find me—even though Jill Zarin, who was also at the party, could have told them how to contact me. Ten months later they get my audition tape and realize I'm the person they have been looking for.

A few weekends later, I'm at my house in the Hamptons when I get a call from the producer telling me they want me on the show and they have a contract for me to sign. I say, "That's great, but before I sign anything I would like to see the demo tape."

She says, "Sorry, but we can't do that."

I don't say no, but I don't back down, "Really? I don't think I can consider doing the show without seeing the demo tape. I don't think I can sign the contract."

She puts me on hold and in a few moments she comes back and says, "Okay, what's your address?" Score one for Ramona. They FedEx the demo tape to me in the Hamptons and it's totally adorable. It opens with Avery who says, "I'm Avery and this is my mom, Ramona." I'm happy with how they capture my energy and portray my family so I decide to do the show.

A few days later, I'm playing tennis with Jill Zarin at my house and she says, "You know, I'm gonna be doing a reality show for a cable channel."

I go, "Really? I got offered a show, too."

It's not until the following week when we meet to play tennis again that we even realize we've been chosen for the same show. When I tell her I got them to send me the demo tape, she's like, "Why didn't I think of that?"

After they send me the contract, I start having second thoughts; *I don't really have time for this. I don't need to be famous. I'm already popular with my friends. I already have a successful business. I'm married. I have my daughter. I have a full life. I don't need this stress in my life. What do I need to take this on for?* I contact Bravo and tell them I'm out.

A few days later, Mario is off playing tennis with Avery, so I decide to get together with a girlfriend. Polo is huge in the Hamptons during the summer. It's kind of like field hockey played on horseback. I'm not a huge fan of the game, but I like to network and people watch. I make some calls and a friend of mine gets us into the VIP tent, where we run into one of the Bravo producers.

She says, "Ramona, I don't understand why you're not doing the show."

I'm a little taken aback that they still want me, but I reply, "I can't do the show because I just don't have time."

Immediately, she starts giving me the hard sell, "It's just an hour or two, once or twice a week. We'll work around your schedule."

Assuming they are looking for an über socialite New York housewife, I argue, "I don't really do all those big charity events anymore. I'm older than Jill. I've done those huge benefits for two hundred, three hundred people. That's not where I'm at anymore."

"That's okay. We don't need that from you."

"I prefer to do dinner parties for fifteen, thirty people tops," I explain.

"Okay, great. We can film that," she insists.

"No, you don't get it. My friends don't want to be filmed," and then, feeling self-conscious, I add, "I'll be boring."

She looks at me and says, "Ramona, since when are you ever boring?"

Then, something clicks in my head. I have been encouraging Mario to build a website to drive business to his company.

I have always believed that business is like a shark; you have to keep moving. If you stop, you die. He has been reluctant because he's always used sales reps, but recently he agreed to give it a shot. We decide that the website should have a different name from the family business, so we call it "True Faith Jewelry" in honor of the inspiring advice my mother gave me when I was a young girl. I decide to do the show as a way to showcase Mario's True Faith Jewelry website.

That night, Mario and I sit down with Avery at the dinner table and tell her, "Avery, we have an opportunity to do this reality show. We'll be in the public eye, but we're not doing it to be famous or popular. We're doing it to help your father's company develop a new business. We're doing it to bring more exposure to the website."

So we did the show. That first season was only supposed to be six episodes but it ended up being nine with the Reunion and Lost Footage episodes. From the beginning, I had a gut feeling that we would average a million viewers. They all thought I was nuts, but I turned out to be right. I knew the show would be a huge success.

Years later, Avery told me that when people would talk to her about the show, especially when they were criticizing something I did that they didn't agree with, her response was always, "My mom does the show for business. It was a business move for her and my father to develop True Faith Jewelry. And now she has other businesses that she's developed because of it."

That's really why I did the show, to help my husband. And then I quickly realized that it was an amazing opportunity for me, too. I was getting burned out doing the closeouts and it was time for me to try something new. The first opportunity that came my way was a chance to promote the skincare line I had been developing for some time. I partnered with a top chemist and it really works. It's made my skin look fifteen years younger. I didn't put it out in stores, or do that much marketing for it. I mostly did it to show Avery how to take a business from beginning to end. Then I did an HSN Jewelry line, which was a dream come true for me. Ultimately, I was even able to develop my own wines, Ramona Pinot Grigio and Ramona Merlot.

One of the biggest benefits of doing *Housewives* has been that it has allowed me to show my daughter that you can find business opportunities anywhere and at any age. Here I was in my fifties and all these doors were opening up for me.

• 4 •

Previously, on *The Real Housewives of New York City* . . .

I FIRST MEET ALEX MCCORD at Townhouse, David Burke's innovative restaurant on the Upper East Side. My first impression: this woman is a boring Stepford wife. Judgmental? Yes. At this point in my life I have a tendency make to snap judgments based on first impressions, but this is something about myself that I am about to learn that I need to change.

It's the fall of 2007 and we have just begun filming the first season of *The Real Housewives of New York City.* I already know or have met all of my castmates, with the exception of Alex. The executives at Bravo have planned for us to meet a bit later in the season. But, as often happens in reality television, it doesn't quite work out that way.

Mario and I have just finished a romantic dinner together and are about to leave the restaurant, when I hear Jill Zarin's raspy voice coming from over by the bar. She is waiting to be seated with her reserved, soft-spoken husband, Bobby. Beside them at the bar is a lanky, fair-skinned blonde and a flamboyantly dressed, animated man with closely cropped ginger hair. For a moment, I wonder if Jill has replaced her "gay husband" Brad, but then I see the man affectionately caressing the blonde's slender back.

Oh my God, I think to myself as I scrunch my face in distaste, *are they a couple?*

Mario and I walk over to the bar and say hello. Jill, who prides herself on connecting people, introduces us to the couple.

"Ramona," she says, "I'd like you to meet Alex McCord—who will be filming the show with us—and her lovely husband, Simon."

I am taken aback. *This* is Alex and Simon. The same Alex and Simon with whom I will be spending the next few months filming. Now that I'm seeing them in person, I suspect the reason Bravo wanted us to meet *after* we started filming was so that they could capture my initial reaction to them on camera. Too late.

"Nice to meet you," I say cordially to Alex as I kiss her on the cheek.

Alex opens her mouth to speak and I hear a grating, Australian accent. Although I may have had one too many cocktails, I know that voice doesn't belong to Alex. Suddenly, Simon is standing up and talking to me. He drones on, and on, and on. I'm not even listening to the words coming out of his mouth. I cannot believe that he won't let his wife get a single word in.

I interject enthusiastically, "So, Alex, are you excited about filming the show?"

She opens her mouth to respond, but Simon speaks over her and answers the question himself. Alex doesn't seem bothered by his interruption. Quite the opposite. To me, she seems like a puppet sitting on her ventriloquist's lap, content to simply sit in the background, smile, and nod her head in agreement. She says nothing.

My head is spinning . . . and it's not from too many cocktails. I'm annoyed by their seemingly codependent dynamic and I don't even understand why. I try to tell myself to stop judging people I don't even know. *How can you jump to conclusions about Alex based on this one encounter?* I ask myself. But I can't help it. It bothers me when I perceive a woman is married to a man who doesn't let her talk and directs her every move. Suddenly, I see the connection. Their relationship reminds me of my parents' awful marriage, a one-sided partnership where the woman is completely dependent on the man. The way Alex and Simon interact with one another has hit a huge nerve. Right or wrong, it's personal for me and I'm completely turned off. I do not like them.

"Mario," I say hastily, "we have to go."

On the way home, Mario and I discuss the encounter.

"That was awkward," I say, working myself up into a frenzy. "I can't believe that Bravo would cast that woman. She has no personality. She's completely nondescript. She's boring."

Mario tries to calm me down. "Maybe it was just awkward because you ladies weren't supposed to meet yet."

"I don't care if we weren't supposed to meet yet," I snap. "It doesn't change the fact that she doesn't appear to be a strong, independent housewife like the rest of us." I pause, roll my eyes, and inhale deeply, "This is going to be a long season."

LOOKING BACK, I now understand that comparing Alex and Simon's marriage with my mother and father's wasn't fair or even rational. Who was I to judge this couple based on one brief encounter at a restaurant bar? For all I knew, Alex was just nervous or shy, or maybe Jill had told her stories that prevented her from warming up to me. It doesn't really matter *why* she was so reserved; my reaction says more about me at that time than it does about Alex and Simon. At that point in my life, and sometimes even to this day, my unresolved issues often clouded my judgment and blurred my vision when it came to friendships, especially with my fellow Housewives. For the next seven seasons, my relationships with the women on the show, my reactions and behavior—good and bad—would play out on television before millions of viewers. Although it has been a long bumpy road, being on the show has been a tremendous learning experience and I have forged friendships that I will cherish for the rest of my life.

While I was very excited to do the show, that first season was difficult for me because I had a lot of stress at home that no one knew about. Mario was very ill during the first months of filming. He was having issues with his business and it had worn him down to the point where it was seriously impacting his health. Meanwhile, I wanted the show to be successful, but I was worried that the other women Bravo had cast weren't going to be entertaining enough. I didn't know Bethenny or Alex very well, but what little I had seen of Alex seemed boring. I had known Jill for years, and at the time I saw her as a whiny, materialistic Long Islander. LuAnn was always very proper and neutral, like Switzerland. I felt like I needed to amp things up, so between what was going on in my personal life at home and my desire to have a successful show, I took things too far that season and wasn't entirely myself.

The way filming for the show works is that the producers will call me and ask, "What's going on this week, Ramona?" I'll tell them I'm having a dinner party, attending a fashion show, or having lunch with a friend and they'll send a camera crew out to film. Everything we film is real; nothing is ever scripted. No one tells us what to say or what to do. I wanted my first appearance on the show to be something that would showcase me on my own, so I decided to have a cooking party with my friend Pamela Morgan of Flirting with Flavors. I remember Bravo encouraged me to have LuAnn stop by so that I would have another Housewife there, but it never occurred to me that Jill would get upset that she wasn't invited. It was just supposed to be an intimate gathering for a few of my close friends. I had no clue it would turn into a fiasco and become a big story line. I didn't feel like I had done anything wrong, but when that episode aired I came off like a bitch for not inviting Jill. That was my first experience of how being on a reality show can bite you in the ass and get you into trouble. My actions were genuine and in no way did I intend to exclude Jill. I had no idea how it would end up coming across or that she would be offended. Maybe I should have, though, because this wasn't the first time we had this issue. Jill and I have always had a volatile friendship; being on the show has only magnified that dynamic.

I knew Jill socially before we started filming. We both had houses in Southampton, so we played tennis and socialized during the summer. We were friendly, but she wasn't a close friend. For years, every Memorial Day weekend I would throw a party for thirty or forty people, but I never invited Jill. Then one year, I remember her saying she couldn't believe I didn't invite her to my party. The truth is, I much prefer to have an intimate get together than a huge party where I can't talk to all of my guests. Inviting Jill meant I had to expand my guest list to the point that it wasn't going to be an intimate gathering any more, so I ended up having two parties just so I wouldn't hurt her feelings.

Since we are both strong-willed and outspoken, I have learned to take a back seat and to avoid going head-to-head with Jill. It's better to let her be strong first, contain my opinion (which is hard for me to do), and wait until she is more receptive, to offer her my point of view. I find that when I use this approach, we have been able to resolve our issues peacefully and have even ended up learning from one another. Naturally, over the years, there have been many, many times when I could not contain myself and we would go at it. But, at the end of the day, we have tremendous respect for one another.

The other big confrontation that first season was at Bethenny's dinner party. I left early and she was very upset and hurt by that. I remember that I had told the producers that I had a previous commitment and had to leave early, but it seems that information was never passed on. I should have said to Jill and Bethenny directly that I was only coming for part of the evening. I was already frazzled when I got there, so when I saw Simon I just snapped and was bitchy to him. Bethenny took me aside and calmed me down. After that, I came out with a martini to welcome him more graciously—unfortunately that didn't make it into the episode. This is another example of how things backfired on me because I feel my actions were taken out of context. Ultimately, though, it doesn't matter. We're all in this to produce a great show. It isn't scripted. What you see on television is what is really happening in our lives. They can't show everything, so it makes sense for them to choose the most provocative and entertaining moments. That's fine with me because I own my behavior. I'm not perfect. If I react poorly in the moment or if I hurt someone's feelings, I am always willing to apologize and to learn from my mistakes. Life is learning.

The reason I have done *The Real Housewives of New York City* for seven seasons is because I have fun working and interacting with the other women on the show. I don't do it to be famous or popular. I have no interest in being a celebrity, but there's no avoiding a certain amount of fame and notoriety when you appear on a hit television show. Almost immediately after the first episode aired, people began to recognize me in public. I would be shopping at Bloomingdale's and people would come up to me and tell me how much they loved me and loved the show. I remember the first time I realized that I could no longer be anonymous in public. I was picking up a sink at a local plumbing store in Southampton and a man there recognized me. He walked right up to me, told me he loved the show, and peppered me with questions about what was going to happen in the rest of the season. I had no makeup on, my hair was a mess, and I was wearing an old pair of sweats. I was so mortified that I wanted to hide under my new sink. Eventually, I learned to take my unwanted celebrity in stride. But early on when people would stop me on the street, I just felt like shrinking into myself. I would try to hide behind Mario and Avery, but they would say, "Take a picture with them. Talk to your fans." That season I was nominated for Bravo's A-list Drama Queen, which was awarded to the most popular and entertaining female in a reality television series, and I remember one of the producers saying to me, "Ramona, you're the star of this season." I just thought, *what are you talking about? What does that even mean?*

I had no comprehension of how much my life would change. None. When the show first aired I didn't even know what a blog was. Jill was much savvier about following social media and blogs, but I had no idea about any of that. I still try not to read about myself. There are a lot of bloggers out there who are full of hate. For the most part I don't let it affect me, but it was harder for Avery. She was only twelve when the show first aired and at the end of the first season, she said to me, "Mom, there's two sides to you. There's the really sweet and lovable side and then there's your wild side. Why do you have to show that side? Why can't you show more of your other side? Let someone else be out of control." I acted out more that first season because I wanted a good show. I wanted to be entertaining, so I pushed the envelope by being a little over the top.

My being so "out there" bothered Avery, so for Season 2 I tried to rein it in a bit. I watched my Ps and Qs and I was more sedate. I avoided conflict, but I wasn't having as much fun. All of a sudden I went from being highly visible in the foreground to fading into the background. I remember at one point my buyer for HSN said to me, "Where's the Ramona I know and love? Who are you this season?" That's when I realized that I was overcompensating and had swung too far in the other direction. I wasn't being true to myself, which is something that I think a lot of the Housewives struggle with when they first come on the show. I think during those first two seasons LuAnn had the same issue. She was all about being The Countess and projecting this very dignified persona. On the show, she would never do anything racy or controversial, but the LuAnn I came to know off the show is really fun and crazy and wild. She drinks and swears and is a very sexy woman. I do think she eventually got more comfortable showing this side of herself, but in the beginning she was much more reserved on camera.

That season Jill and Bethenny became the dynamic duo, the way Sonja and I are now. At the Season 2 Reunion, I felt like they teamed up against me. I felt attacked and couldn't get out of bed the next day. For the Season 1 Reunion episode, we all had our hair and make up done in one big dressing room, but for this season I remember Jill insisted that none of us see each other before we sat down to film. Then somehow she and Bethenny ended up sharing a dressing room. I assumed she had planned it that way so that she and Bethenny would have time alone together. My experience at that reunion felt very abusive. Almost immediately, I felt like Jill jumped on me about how long I had been working on my skincare line. I didn't even know how to react. At that point, I didn't really have the verbal tactics. When I felt backed into a corner, I would say the wrong thing or just fumfer. Or I would sit there and take it because of the verbal abuse I witnessed as a child. When you have a history of abuse, you tend to shut down when you feel attacked. You don't fight back. You go into a state of numbness. I should have said, "Stop. You're hurting my feelings. What you're saying and how you're treating me isn't right." Now, I'm more in control and I know how to handle myself better, but at the time I just shut down.

I remember people writing in after that episode aired, to say that the way they went after me was vicious. I think Jill is the type of person who can sniff out someone's weaknesses like a dog. I feel like she saw the chink in my armor and pounced. We taped for seven hours that day and the next day I couldn't get out of bed. When I got home, I said to Mario, "I can't do this anymore. Taping these reunions is as painful as giving birth." I remember, he laughed and said, "Well, then the memory of the pain will go away."

After that Reunion episode I did a lot of soul searching. When I decided to sign on for Season 3, I said to my family, "I'm going to be me now. I have to be more expressive and show who I really am. I'm not going to rein myself in." I had finally realized that I needed to be myself, because me as *me* is very entertaining. I'm funny, I'm witty, and I'm upbeat. On the other hand, I also became aware of how my impulsive side could affect the other women on the show. While spontaneity can be a good thing, being impulsive means that you act before you think, which can have the consequence of hurting people's feelings. I can definitely be insensitive, but it is never my intention to hurt anyone.

So for Season 3, I revealed a whole new Ramona. I was determined to be true to myself but I also embraced a philosophy of renewal in all aspects of my life. I cut my hair, renewed my vows with my husband, and started examining my relationships with the other women on the show. I dropped my judgmental attitude about Alex and Simon and we actually ended up developing a meaningful friendship. Initially, it was awkward for me to be around them. I felt as though Alex and Simon had invaded my territory. It takes too much effort to be polite and make small talk with someone I don't like, and I don't know how to fake it and pretend to be friendly, so if they came to an event that I was also attending I just found it easier to leave or go to the other side of the room.

When Simon approached me at the Russell Simmons fashion show and asked me outright why I didn't like him, I was completely taken aback. In retrospect, I'm glad he confronted me because I was able to say exactly what was on my mind. Even though my opinion of him didn't change right away, it cleared a path for a friendship to develop. Now I can see that a big part of why I reacted so negatively to them was in part because they were from Brooklyn. It had a bad connotation for me, but I had buried my memories of going there so deeply that I didn't make the connection right away. When I finally went to Brooklyn, I began to remember the time my mother took us to stay with my grandmother after my father had hit her. Suddenly it became clear to me that I was projecting my own issues onto them.

Once I realized that, it changed everything for me. I stopped judging Alex and Simon and we became very good friends. I came to realize that Alex is a happy, grounded, secure, and self-confident woman. She is not threatened or intimidated by other people's success or achievements. I think we learned a lot from one another during our time together on the show and it was great to watch her come out of her shell. I encouraged to her to become stronger and more outspoken and by the end of Season 3 she had found her voice.

That season was also a turning point in my friendship with Bethenny, beginning with the day we walked across the Brooklyn Bridge. When that episode aired it was very upsetting for me to hear the things I had said to her. I told her that she didn't have any friends and that she would probably screw up her relationship with her then-boyfriend, Jason. Even though our conversation leading up to this moment was heated and we were both exchanging barbs, the bottom line is that she came to me with a situation that was troubling her and she needed my sympathy and support. Instead, I became defensive and lashed out, hitting below the belt, just like my father had done. I had to own up to my behavior and I apologized to Bethenny. We got past it and we are now genuine friends.

Bethenny and I are very similar. We both grew up with a lot of tension in our childhoods. We both had terrible relationships with our fathers. We're both street-smart, ambitious, and self-made. We both got married and had children in our late thirties. There are a lot of parallels there. While walking across the bridge that day, I finally took in the distress and pain she was feeling over her fallout with Jill. I

With Mario and Alex

had never seen her so upset and I was genuinely concerned, which is why I came up with a plan for her to meet with Jill at my house. I was hoping they would hash out their issues and make peace with one another. I really wanted to help them find a way to rebuild their friendship. I knew the situation was causing them both pain and they needed to make amends. Never in a million years did I think they would leave my home without coming to a resolution.

I think that what happened between them was that Jill was resentful that Bravo had offered Bethenny her own show. We all knew it was happening. I remember the plan was for her to film Season 3 with us and then she would start filming her spinoff. Maybe Jill thought it should be the "Jill and Bethenny Show" or that she should have gotten her own show, but I remember her calling me up at my office and asking me not to film with Bethenny. I said to her, "Why would you want to hurt her that way? You know she's on her own and has to support herself. You have a husband. I'm set financially. Why would you stand in her way?" I think she felt that Bethenny was riding our coattails and she was jealous that she would have success on her own. Alex and I confronted her about this during the Reunion episode. At first Jill denied she had done this, but eventually she did admit it. I think Jill is the type of person that if you have something she doesn't have, instead of wishing you well she feels slighted that she's not a part of it. That's just her personality. Although it's often riled me up over the years, I've learned to accept her for who she is.

I do believe that if Jill and Bethenny had more time to talk that day they might have eventually reconciled.

With LuAnn and Sonja

Looking back, I should have left the apartment with LuAnn, so they could have a chance to work things out on their own. I don't think LuAnn was a positive presence that day. She and Jill had recently become close and I think subconsciously she may have felt their new friendship would be threatened if Jill and Bethenny became friends again. I really feel that she inserted herself into the situation and prevented them from finishing their conversation. When Jill walked out that day, the door closed on their friendship for good. This is an issue that would come up again when Sonja and I became so close. I think it's hard for LuAnn to share friends. It's a common mistake we women make; we get possessive and territorial. But women should not feel threatened by other women's friendships. Friends are meant to be shared. There really is enough love to go around.

When Kelly joined us on the show, I knew of her but had never met her. She was very prominent socially because of her ex-husband, the famous French fashion photographer Gilles Bensimon. Before we met, I actually googled her and listened to some of her interviews. She seemed like she was nice and engaging and my initial reaction to her was positive. But the more I got to know her, the more I began to feel that there was no depth to her. I felt like as long as she could talk about children and nail polish and clothes she was fine, but beyond that she didn't seem to have anything substantial to say, so I found having a real conversation with her difficult.

Right away there was friction between Bethenny and Kelly. Where Kelly was a true socialite It Girl, who was always invited to all the A-list parties, Bethenny was this scrappy, self-made street urchin who was working her way to the top. There was a lot of resentment there because they had met a number of times, but Kelly would always act like she didn't remember. And probably Kelly didn't remember because she couldn't have cared less about Bethenny. The tension between them had been simmering since Kelly's infamous I'm-up-here-you're-down-there hand gesture during their confrontation at Brass Monkey, but it blew way the hell up in St. Thomas.

I was about to renew my vows and I thought it would be fun for us to all go away together and celebrate. I had not gone on a girls' trip since I married Mario and I was looking forward to spending time with the ladies. When I picked Sonja up I was so excited I could hardly contain myself. I knew we would feed off each other's positive energy and it was on this trip that *Ramonja* was born. Bethenny's father had just passed away and she had also recently found out she was pregnant, so when she called to say she could go, I was touched. Alex had never been away from her two young boys so I was also really appreciative that she had agreed to come. I knew it would be therapeutic for them both to get away and just relax. I even decided to put aside my issues with Kelly and invited her to come. I was disappointed that Jill and LuAnn didn't join us, but I chose not to dwell on it.

Once we were all together on the yacht, I was so over-the-top happy and excited. We were all getting along chatting and naturally we began talking about our feelings for Jill and how her behavior had been affecting us. This seemed to immediately make Kelly uncomfortable because she kept saying she didn't want to talk about *feelings*. I think Kelly has a hard time conversing in intimate situations, especially when the subject of emotions comes up. The way I see it, if you have no feelings and you cannot talk about them or be in touch with them, then you might as well be a robot. While we were on the yacht, I remember Kelly was on the phone with Jill three or four times a day. She seemed to be

Photo shoot with Kelly Bensimon in St. John

getting increasingly agitated, and I think some of that may have been Jill stirring her up.

For the next part of our trip we stayed at Presidio del Mar, a majestic villa in St. John. I'm not easily impressed, but I have to say this villa was beyond anything I had ever visited or seen. The cameras did not even begin to do it justice. The following morning, Kelly seemed to have calmed down and that day we spent on the beach with her was amazing. She

The ladies in St. John: Kelly, Alex, me, and Sonja

prepared a great lunch and treated us to a fantastic photo shoot. She was at ease in her own element and was a pleasure to be with. But at dinner that night something in her snapped. Suddenly, out of nowhere, she seemed to be in the midst of a major meltdown. I don't know what caused it. Maybe she was just out of her comfort zone, but we all wondered if she had forgotten to take her medication or if perhaps she had mixed some kind of medication with too much alcohol. We were drinking tequila on the beach that day and she doesn't really drink. Tequila makes me nutty, so maybe it had a strange affect on her. I personally felt the meltdown was twenty times worse than what they aired on television. We were so concerned that we called Jill that night. I told her, "Kelly needs you. She's going to be on a plane. You should meet her in New York." Even Bethenny got on the phone and said, "Jill, this is not about the show; we're worried about Kelly." But, instead of meeting her friend and helping her at the airport, Jill decided to show up in at the villa the next day. I guess she thought she was going to swoop in and have some kind of reconciliation with Bethenny, but it was too little too late.

Bethenny and I have come a long way. But it hasn't always been easy for us. She has this way of making her digs through her sense of humor, so you almost don't realize that she's insulting you. That's her schtick and she's excellent at it. She comes across like a comedienne, but her words can be quite biting. Part of our confrontation at the Season 2 Reunion had to do with my response to a biting comment she made when I was giving her dating advice. I was hurt by what she said, so in my blog I made the dig '*why buy the milk if you can get the cow for free?*' in reference to her having previously lived with boyfriends outside of marriage. She got really pissed off about that. I remember she called me up and she actually scared the crap out of me, and then I felt threatened when she and Jill went after me at the Reunion. She seemed like a cat ready to scratch my eyes out. It takes a lot to shake me up, but Bethenny's a person that you just don't cross. She can dish it out but she can't take it.

With Bethenny at her birthday party

We're in a much different place now. I think it's because my walls are down and I'm more communicative. The Ramona I am today might have said, "Come on, Bethenny, don't take this so seriously. I'm sorry you're offended," but back then I panicked and retreated. I literally went under my covers like when I was a child and my parents would fight. Now, I handle things differently. I've learned to communicate better. Early into the filming of Season 7, Bethenny and I got into a huge fight. But I realized very quickly, *what are we fighting about? This is ridiculous.* The old Ramona would've said, *Okay, we had a fight. I'm angry at her, she's angry at me. So be it.* The issue would have festered and we might have damaged our friendship for good. Being the person I am now, I decided to go see her to try and reconcile right away. Of course, she got even angrier but I kept calm and approached her again and, in the end, we made up. Sometimes people are just angry. Not at you, but about their situation. In the past, I never saw things that way. I would take things way too personally, but I've evolved.

Recently LuAnn said to me, "Ramona, you're so warm and fuzzy now." Who would ever have thought LuAnn would call *me* warm and fuzzy? I think that going through what I went through with my marriage falling apart has made me a different person. When you're emotionally hurt like that, when you're betrayed by your husband, it makes you more vulnerable. You can retreat or you can learn from it. It was a learning experience. Not a good one, but life is learning.

What is a friend? A friend is someone who is there for you through the good, the bad, and the ugly, someone who allows you to express yourself, and someone who forgives you for your mistakes. No one is perfect. I know I still have a lot of growing to do, but I am trying. I am a very emotional person. I'm *Ramotional.* There is nothing wishy-washy about me. I am very passionate. There are no grey areas with me. I am an extremist. I argue hard and I make up harder. I ignite quickly, but when a disagreement is over, it's over. I do not hold grudges because life is too short.

• 5 •

Look Good, Feel Better, Act Your Best

IT'S MARCH OF 2009. I am sitting in a green room in Tampa, Florida. In less than thirty minutes, I will be on live television showcasing my new art deco jewelry line on HSN. I am so excited and nervous, I actually have butterflies in my stomach like I'm about to go on a first date. I take a sip of sparkling water and a handful of unsalted almonds. I need to calm down.

Although I have had cameras following me around through two seasons of filming for *Real Housewives*, there is something about live television that freaks me out. For starters, there is no editing. And, as any of my fellow Housewives will tell you, I need editing. First and foremost, there's the issue of *when* to speak. I don't have a problem finding things to say, but I do have a hard time taking direction. I'm worried about knowing when *I* should talk and when I should let the host talk. I am wearing a cumbersome, uncomfortable earpiece that shouts out production directives in my ear, while I am supposed to be talking and staring directly into a camera. Oh, crap, I hadn't even thought of that yet. Although I've become comfortable with having cameras around me, I'm not at all used to looking directly into them. I am completely out of my element. This experience is totally new for me and, like everything I do, I want it to be a success.

Despite my nerves, tonight is a dream come true. Having my own jewelry line sold on HSN is something I have always wanted to do. I wish my mother was still alive to share it with me. She would have been so proud. She is the reason I have always believed in myself and had the confidence to take risks in business.

It's 10:00 p.m. I am perched at a high Formica countertop. I feel like I am sitting at a bar, except there are no cocktails, no glass of Pinot Grigio. Instead, there are cameras and lights all around me. On the table in front of me is a tall white jewelry stand and a small gift box that contains a pair of earrings that I intend to present as a gift to the host during the program. Sitting next to me is Colleen, my host for the evening. I am so glad that HSN gave me Colleen for my first show. Not only is she the type of woman that you'd want to go shopping with, but this enthusiastic, engaging saleswoman could sell ice in a blizzard.

The show begins. Colleen introduces me and my line of jewelry. While she models a pink sapphire ring encrusted with diamonds on her perfectly manicured hand, I am supposed to interject with information about my designs and the vision for my collection. But when?

"Ramona, Camera 1. Look at Camera 1," my earpiece shouts.

I look at Camera 1, smile, and begin talking, "I wanted my designs to look like fabulous, expensive, pieces of heirloom estate jewelry that never go out of style. Timeless, elegant and classic jewelry that you can pass down to your daughter."

Just as I am about to continue with my next thought, I hear my earpiece again, *Ramona, stop hogging the microphone!* No, wait, that's not the earpiece, it's just the nagging voice in my head. Now, Colleen is saying, "Yes, this jewelry looks very expensive, but it is so affordable. For only $300 dollars—or five payments of $60—you get this gorgeous ring that looks like it costs $30,000."

"Ramona, Camera 2," my earpiece whispers.

I stare into Camera 2, "Yes, and it looks just like the pieces that I have seen on Madison Avenue or at estate auctions. The best part is that you can wear it to a black tie event or to a luncheon on a Saturday afternoon."

I begin to relax and feel more at ease. I can't believe this is happening. I can't believe I am live on HSN selling *my* designs. To think, if I hadn't been motivated to renew my career, I would not be sitting in this chair right now. The earpiece interrupts my thoughts again. I feel like a timid kid in school who didn't do her homework and doesn't want to get called on by the teacher. The difference is that I actually *did* do my homework; I just don't want to sound like I'm bragging about my creations. As I try to think of something inspirational and humble to say, the magic earpiece tells Colleen sternly, "Open the box on the countertop."

Prior to the show, I had placed a gift box on the countertop for Colleen. I always like giving people I work with a little present when I first meet them. It's a small gesture that shows I appreciate the time they are spending on me. Trust me, it goes a long way.

Colleen delicately opens the box. It contains a pair of elegant prasiolite, pale green amethyst, drop earrings, surrounded by diamonds. "Ramona, thank you," she says. "They are gorgeous." Judging from the look in her eyes, she genuinely loves the earrings. Her priceless reaction is perhaps the best salesmanship of the night.

The show is over. The earrings that I gifted to Colleen sell out in minutes. We sell out of a lot of other pieces too, far surpassing HSN's sales expectations. I have fulfilled a dream.

Because I am able to recognize opportunities and I'm not afraid to take risks, I have always been very successful at everything I do. But one thing I am about to learn the hard way is that sometimes you can take on too much, and if you allow yourself to be spread too thin something has to give . . .

Creating my own line of Jewelry for the HSN was a dream come true. Ever since I started working with Mario on the True Faith Jewelry website, I wanted to branch out and create my own designs. I researched the latest selling trends in retail and worked with a factory that had on-staff designers to create beautiful pieces inspired by the art deco estate jewelry that I love. Because I had the ambition and courage to pick up the phone and cold call the Vice President of Jewelry Merchandising at HSN, soon I was selling my own jewelry line on live television and through the Internet.

After twenty years running my first company, I was reenergized by all the new business opportunities that were coming my way. Some women like to shop and organize charity luncheons but I prefer making business deals. My advice to people has always been that to be truly successful, you have to love what you do. I have always been deeply passionate about all my product lines. However, I have learned that it is possible to take on too much—even for me.

I already had the skincare line, the TrueFaithJewelry.com line, and now my HSN jewelry was taking off. Meanwhile, my name was becoming synonymous with Pinot Grigio. Like Popeye with spinach. I enjoy a glass of wine at night or with dinner and my go-to drink has always been a Pinot Grigio. It's a fairly inexpensive wine so when you order it by the glass at a restaurant you know it will taste fine. You're less likely to be able to order a great tasting wine, like a Cabernet or a Montrachet, by the glass. Pinots are light so you can drink them with or without food, and generally you don't have to worry about the year or the brand. I became known for loving Pinot Grigio on the show. On the show, at parties or events you'll hear me asking, "Where's my Pinot Grigio? Do you have my Pinot Grigio?" Eventually, wherever I went, people knew: Pinot Grigio for Ramona.

By the time the third season had aired, I was getting thousands of tweets and messages asking about my favorite Pinot or what brand of wine to buy as a gift for a relative. I always shied away from naming a specific brand because I think in the back of my mind I had already planted a seed to develop my own wine. When a California company approached me to partner with it to develop a Pinot Grigio, I was excited by the idea but I had my reservations.

I told Mario, "I don't think I should do it. I don't really want to do a wine from California. I believe Pinot Grigio should be from Italy."

And he said, "Fine, then you should do that."

I said, "What do you mean do *that*?"

He looked at me, "Ramona, you're a smart business-woman. You'll figure out how to do it the way you want. This is what you do. Just do it."

I thought the idea was crazy so I put it out of my mind. A few nights later I was in East Hampton attending my good friend Vittorio Assaf's opening for the new location of his restaurant Serafina. There was press milling around outside and one of the reporters called out to me, "Hey, Ramona, when I saw you were on the list I told them they better have Pinot Grigio for you." As soon as Vittorio saw me, he walked right over and said, "Ramona, I have Pinot Grigio for you." I couldn't get away from it. Ramona and Pinot Grigio just go together. I told Vittorio that I had been thinking about developing my own Pinot and he offered to introduce me to his sommelier.

That August, Avery was on the committee for Operation Smile, an organization that provides free surgeries to repair cleft lips and palates for children around the world. They were doing a benefit in the Hamptons and needed some wine, so I got in touch with the Opici Family, one of the most respected wine importers in the country. I had used them for other events, so we already had a relationship. At the end of the call, I asked if they would be interested in

Signings for Ramona Pinot Grigio

doing a Pinot Grigio with me and they said, "Absolutely, let's set up a meeting." From there, things happened fairly quickly. They sent me different blends to sample and we started developing the wine. I researched how other bottles were labeled and packaged. I didn't like the big chateaux and distracting images you see on a lot of wine bottles. I wanted something clean and simple, so I decided to just use my name in black over gold on a clean white label. I designed the label, the cap, and even the cartons the wines are

BOTTLE SIGNING & TASTING
SATURDAY, AUGUST 20th
4pm to 5pm
RAMONA
PINOT GRIGIO
COME & MEET
RAMONA
2010
DELLE VENEZIE
PINOT GRIGIO

packed in. When you go into a liquor store, particularly the larger ones in the suburbs, they stack the cartons and it becomes a display, so you can't just package your wine in plain cardboard boxes. I love the way Moët & Chandon is all yellow-gold with black, so my cartons are inspired by Moët. By the time we started filming Season 4, my Ramona Pinot Grigio was ready to go.

The best part of the trip to St. John the year before was that I had rekindled my friendship with Sonja. We've known each other for thirty years and she always puts a smile on my face. Her positivity and zest for life always help to diffuse all the crazy situations we Housewives get into. Sonja is a woman who enjoys life and has had the best that life offers. When she came on the show she was like a breath of fresh air, so I went into Season 4 feeling energized and excited. Unfortunately, it turned out to be one of the most difficult seasons for me.

I had been looking forward to filming with Cindy Barshop, who I had recommended bringing onto the show. We had really good energy before we started filming, but once we were on camera she seemed to have all this animosity towards me. Meanwhile, with Bethenny now off the show, I felt like Jill came gunning for me. It was horrible. She seemed jealous that I was showcasing my Pinot Grigio and I felt that she was trying to make me look like I have a drinking problem. Television is a powerful medium and if a lie is repeated often enough people will start to believe it. I felt like the more she accused me of having a drinking problem, the more viewers believed her. For the record: I do not have a drinking problem nor have I ever struggled with addiction of any kind. I am an adult, I work hard and play hard, but I know my limits and I am never out of control. You rarely see Jill drinking on the show and I've heard that the reason for this is that she has had problems with substance abuse in the past. I have always respected her privacy, so for her to publicly accuse of me of having a drinking problem, which is not true, was very upsetting to me.

It all came to a head at Jill's charity event to raise awareness of bullying, which is ironic since I felt as if I was the one being bullied. When ladies go to a charity luncheon and pay $200 a ticket, they expect a glass of wine with their meal. Jill's assistant had asked me to donate some of my Pinot as there was no wine donor for the luncheon. I couldn't sponsor the event because I had a very limited supply in from Italy at that time, but I wanted to help. I carried a heavy, twelve-bottle case of wine in heels over to the event through the pouring rain, but somehow my gesture was completely misinterpreted. In that episode you see me drinking, but they kept showing me with the same glass. It looks like I was drinking more than I was. Jill criticized me on the show for drinking a glass of wine at noon, but meanwhile she was serving these heavy-duty vodka martinis at the same lunch. I think the real reason she came after me that season was that she was resentful that I had come out with another product and she didn't have one. I had my HSN Jewelry, the TrueFaithJewelry.com line, I had my skincare line, and now I was debuting my Ramona Pinot Grigio. I think she just couldn't be supportive. I call it *Jillousy*. I started to feel like she had decided to make me her punching bag and that she was trying to turn all the girls against me.

Morocco, Season 4

Meanwhile, I wasn't getting along with the head producer in the field. We were like oil and water. He was the type of man who I felt just didn't like powerful women. I have a strong voice and I refuse to apologize for it. He and I would butt heads all the time. I felt that he didn't like the connection between Sonja and I and that he wanted to pit us against one another. I reached my breaking point during the trip to Morocco. I felt that the psychic who claimed Mario was cheating on me was a setup. I can't begin to speculate who was behind

Real Housewives riding camels!

it, but I don't believe she was a real psychic. Mario and I had just renewed our vows the year before and at that point our relationship was totally on track. Then, when Jill and I had our big fight, I just fell apart. I actually remember saying to the producer, "You broke me. Are you happy? You broke me." I have always had a very strong spirit, but after the strain of that season I felt broken. I was miserable to the

Ramonja in Morocco

point where I almost told them I wasn't going to do the show the following season. I couldn't be myself around him. They were supposed to get a new producer for Season 5, but they didn't so I asked not to have him around when I was filming because he gave me negative energy.

That year I threw myself into my businesses. In April of 2011, I was honored as Entrepreneur of the Year by the

Women's Venture Fund and the following November I was named "Mogul of the Year" at the Stevie Awards for Women in Business. I was doing the skincare line, I was doing HSN, I was doing True Faith, I still had RMS Fashions, I was creating a Merlot, and I was traveling all over the country doing signings for Ramona Pinot Grigio. I was working too much and spreading myself too thin. I remember carrying around five different plastic folders, in different colors, one for each business to keep everything straight. On top of all that I still had to be a mother to Avery, a wife to Mario, and maintain my two homes. I was killing myself, working nonstop. Looking back, I think I was hiding in my businesses because it kept me detached from my emotional state and from the people around me. Some people go after drugs, sex, or, alcohol. For me, diving into business after business was a way to avoid getting close to people and to keep them at arm's length. I was beginning to see that my business ambitions were impacting how I dealt with my personal relationships.

When you take on too much, something has to give. My True Renewal skincare line was a fabulous product. It will literally change your skin in four weeks, but because I was doing so many things I didn't have time to market it. I also took my eye off the HSN line. In business you have to be hands-on, but at that point I was traveling so much for my Pinot Grigio that I wasn't paying enough attention to how my jewelry was being priced. I had an assistant, but I was trying to do it all because I'm a take-charge person. For my initial line the average piece was retailing for $300, but by the end, out of fifteen pieces, ten were priced at $1,000-plus. When we were developing the line, I kept asking about the prices but I remember the buyer would tell me not to worry about it. So I just looked at the sketches they had produced from photos of pieces I had shown them and picked the ones that I liked. Then all of a sudden I had a product line ready to go on air that the average piece was priced so high it wasn't going to sell. The bottom line is, I should never have approved anything unless I knew the price first. Even *I* wouldn't pay a thousand dollars for my own jewelry and I'm in the top 1% of wealth. The philosophy behind the line was that the jewelry looked like it was worth thousands but only cost hundreds, but once I took my eye off the ball, my product line suffered. The truth is, you can't do it all. That's what I was learning.

In the fall of 2012, I finally hit the wall. I had been on the road, traveling for Ramona Pinot Grigio twenty-five times a year. It burned me out. I got very sick and it turned into a very important wake-up call. I was already filming the Reunion episode for Season 5 and I went on a day trip to Columbus, Ohio. When I came back to New York, I went shopping for a dress with my girlfriend at an upscale boutique on Madison Avenue. I was so exhausted that I had to lie down on the store's couch. You know me, I'm Miss Energy, so this was a serious red flag. My girlfriend said to me, "Ramona, you need to see a doctor. Something isn't right with you."

I went to the doctor and when she asked me to shut my eyes, I lost my equilibrium and collapsed. Fortunately, the doctor caught me before I hit the floor. I was diagnosed with vertigo and an acute inner ear infection. For the next three months, I had such bad vertigo that I could barely function. I couldn't concentrate enough to read a book or write. I could barely even think straight. I was a mess. I took steroids for three months and by Christmas I was starting to get better, but then one night I started to feel strange again. I was in the bathroom and when Mario walked in, I said to him, "I don't feel right." I shut my eyes to see if I would fall, just as I did at the doctor's office. I should've held on to something, because I collapsed and banged my head on the hard marble floor, just barely missing the bathtub. That brought it all back again. That's when I finally realized that I needed to take a step back, calm down, and regroup. Eventually I did get better, but I'm still sensitive to loud noises and once in a blue moon I still get slight vertigo.

After I got sick, I realized that the way I had been living was absurd. Every week I was on a plane going somewhere to do a signing. My health was seriously at risk and my husband was beginning to feel neglected. I decided not to travel for the Pinot Grigio anymore. I spent more time with Mario and focused on helping Avery prepare to go away to college. At that time she had been accepted early decision to Emory University in Atlanta and Michigan State University. Getting a child in New York City into a college costs a small fortune. Between ACTs and SATs, you can spend as much on tutors as you do for private school. It's insane. Helping her get through the application process and decide where she wanted to go was stressful enough.

I did one more HSN show after I got sick, but that was it. I can always go back to it at some point in the future, but I realized that I had already accomplished so much. What more did I need to prove? Yes, I love working. I truly am an entrepreneur at heart. I'd rather make money than go to a girls' lunch. I get more pleasure out of making a business deal than I do from buying a new piece of jewelry. But I had reached a point where it had turned into escapism. Some people hide in drugs, alcohol, or sex. I was escaping into my work. I became irritable and impatient because I was on overload. I'd wake up in the middle of the night and start answering emails or jotting down ideas. I was running five businesses and two homes, planning vacations, being social, working with Avery to get her into a top college, entertaining, going out, having dinner parties, and planning Christmases and Easters—all while filming a reality television show for six straight seasons. I have been working since I was fourteen years old. I needed a break. So I decided to concentrate on my family and on my health. I started working out more, I took cooking lessons, and was eating healthier.

I still love business, but now I only take on projects where I'm part of a team so every decision doesn't fall solely on my shoulders. I still love doing the Ramona Pinot and Ramona Merlot, but I don't do all the traveling for it. In December of 2014, I partnered with my friend, restaurateur Peter Guimaraes, to open AOA Bar and Grill, a 6,000 square-foot, 190-seat restaurant in Tribeca. Peter approached me and said, "I think AOA would be a great match for you." I decided to get involved because I felt like it would be fun change in pace from everything I had been doing and a great way to display my wines. AOA is a lively sports bar that is conducive to meeting and talking. It's a fun, relaxed place where you can hang out with friends, meet people, and network. I personally feel when you go to a restaurant it's more fun in the bar area. Who wants to sit at a table alone in the corner?

I've also been focusing on helping my daughter become a businesswoman in her own right. Since she was a little girl, I have involved her in many ways and she has learned first-hand by watching me from start to finish in all my ventures. When Avery was applying to colleges, the President of Nickelodeon Networks, Cyma Zarghami, came to speak at her high school and said, "To be successful in business you need to love what you do." She came home so excited, squealing, "Mom, that's what *you* always tell me!" Avery has grown into a sharp, ambitious young woman and she has been approached by different companies who want her to be the face of their product. My job is to help guide her and ensure that, no matter what business she decides to become involved with, her health and happiness come first.

Healthy on the Inside, Beautiful on the Outside . . .

IT IS SUMMER 2009. I walk into Oscar Blandi Salon. The stations are set up in a long row, and the entire salon is bathed in natural light and subdued earth tones. I look at myself in the mirror. Although I generally look and feel exhausted when I go to the salon, today I am in a playful and daring mood. In the back of my mind, I have a purpose. I want to do something different.

I walk past the exposed brick walls and sit in Oscar's

swivel chair. I first met Oscar Blandi in 2007. *Harper's Bazaar* was doing a spread on *The Real Housewives of New York City* and Oscar was the head hairstylist. I was impressed by how he was able to handle us boisterous and demanding ladies on that long shoot and he has been cutting, coloring, and styling my hair ever since. I figured if he can take on all the Housewives together, he can certainly handle me on my own.

I take a sip of Pellegrino and start talking, "I feel like doing something different today. I want a new look. What do you suggest?"

He looks stunned. "Really? What's going on?" He runs his fingers through my long blonde hair, "I know how much you love your long locks."

"I just feel like it's time for a new look. I'm going through a process of renewal in different aspects of my life. I'm renewing my relationship with my husband, my daughter and my girlfriends. Why not renew my appearance, too? I want to make sure my inner self matches my outer appearance."

He smiles devilishly, "Well, how short are you willing to go?"

I laugh. His question reminds me of being on an awkward high school date, where the guy asks if you're willing to go to third base. I look around the salon and spot a stunning picture of the vivacious and lovable Kelly Ripa on the cover of a magazine. I turn to look at myself in the mirror and place one hand on top of each shoulder. "Right to here," I say.

"Ramona, are you sure?" he asks. I nod my head. He continues, "Okay. We won't make it so drastic. I will keep the front of your hair the same—long layers and the bang—and just cut and layer the back. I promise I will make it short, sexy and sassy."

"Cut away," I insist.

When the steels scissors hit my long locks, I start to freak out. I have had long hair since I was sixteen years old. I wonder if I have just made a huge mistake. Maybe I shouldn't have been so bold. I try to calm down. I close my eyes and put my complete faith in Oscar. I trust him. I tell myself that I can handle this. After all, it's just hair. It will grow back . . . eventually.

"All finished," Oscar says happily.

I stare into the illuminated mirror. My eyes open wide. I barely recognize the woman looking back at me. I feel like a new person inside and out. The woman getting her hair done a few stations over says, "Wow, I love your hair. You look so much younger. You look fabulous."

"I'll take it," I say, "who doesn't want to look younger?"

I run my hands though my soft, short, sassy hair. I actually feel lighter. I feel free. As I open the salon door and walk out onto Madison Avenue, I want to scream, *hey everybody, look at me. This is the new Ramona.*

THE PHYSICAL ACT of cutting my long hair was a symbolic moment in my life. After my father passed away, I let go of a lifetime of negative energy and suppressed depression. In cutting off all those inches, I was actually severing ties to a past that had weighed me down for most of my life. My new look was an outward, physical sign that I was beginning a new chapter in my life and taking control of my destiny. I was setting myself free and opening myself up to new experiences. I was saying to myself—and to the world—*I am a new woman. I am no longer going to hide behind my long blonde hair. I am renewing myself inside and out.* I am a firm believer that how you look on the outside should reflect what you feel on the inside. Cutting my hair short was symbolic of where I was at in my life at that point. I was going through a period of self-reflection and renewal and to honor that I wanted to radically transform my whole look.

A few years later I found myself in a much different place than where I was that day at Oscar's salon. I was rundown from working too much and it had taken a toll on my health. We took almost eighteen months off between filming Seasons 5 and Season 6, time I had needed to regroup and focus on my health and my family. Avery left for college in the fall of 2013, while we were in the middle of filming Season 6. No mother is ever ready for her child to go off to college. It meant I could no longer go into her room every night and every morning to kiss her. I could no longer cuddle up in her bed with her, or chitchat as we picked out an outfit for her wear out with her friends. I was overwhelmed by a sense of loss. Obviously, I was happy for Avery, but I was also sad for me. Part of being a mother is letting go, but that doesn't mean it's easy. Avery leaving the house was a very difficult transition for me, and then almost immediately my marriage of twenty-one years began to fall apart. I was completely blindsided by the revelation that Mario had been cheating on me. I never even saw it coming. It would have been so easy to give in to depression and let my body fall apart, but I decided not to allow that to happen. I started working with a personal trainer and eating healthier. I actually look better now than I did ten years ago.

My fit body

I always strive be in the best physical shape that I can be for my age. Some women treat themselves to expensive shoes or purses, I prefer to spend my money on ways to stop the aging clock as long as possible. When we use makeup artists for the show they are always amazed at the quality and youthfulness of my skin. Using anti-aging skincare products on a regular basis helps with wrinkles, pore size, elasticity, hydration, and age spots. Botox injections are an instant, temporary fix for wrinkles that typically lasts three to four months. Anti-aging skincare revitalizes the skin and improves its texture, something that Botox does not do. It also minimizes wrinkles. I've tried Botox, but I believe a good skincare regime is much more effective over time. That was a big reason why I had been inspired to develop my own skincare line.

I feel plastic surgery should be put off as long as possible. If you take care of your body by working out regularly and eating right, you will look naturally younger for longer. That's just a fact. I have done extensive research into anti-aging skincare and nonsurgical options for maintaining a youthful face and body and, for the most part, when it comes to preserving the skin on the face and neck it boils down to this: use SPF 30 sunscreen and always wear a hat in the sun. Eventually, however, most women as they age do get brown spots or freckles, particularly on the face, no matter how much sunblock they use. That is why the Intense Pulsed Light (IPL) machine is so great. It uses a broad-spectrum light source to erase all kinds of sun damage. You're in and out in an hour. Youre face will be red and sometimes your skin will crust over, so you're not going want to go to a black tie that night, but it's a minimally invasive procedure with virtually no pain.

For most women, as we get older cellulite becomes a harsh reality and exercise is only half the battle. As our skin ages and loses collagen and elastin, it's replaced by clusters of fat cells just below the surface of the skin. When those fat cells increase in size, they bulge to create that unsightly cottage cheese look, particularly on our thighs and buttocks. A lot of women are quick to go under the knife, but there are so many alternatives to plastic surgery. My good friend, Dr. Sharon Giese, offers a treatment in her office called VASER Shape, which eliminates unwanted fat cells and reduces the appearance of cellulite through the use of ultrasound and massage therapy. Studies on these treatments have shown deep tissue massage can break down fibrous bands of fat, aiding circulation and resulting in an improvement on how the skin appears. I have tried this non-surgical, painless procedure and had excellent results.

I've never had any surgery on my face, but I recently did have my breasts done. While filming Season 7, the girls kept asking me if I had them done, but I just kept telling them, "Oh, no. I've been doing push ups and because I lost weight it made my breasts look a little bigger." At that point I hadn't decided if I wanted to tell anyone, but I've always been honest about the work I've had done and I don't believe it's anything to be ashamed of. I feel good about my body. I've worked hard to maintain a youthful look, and I'm proud that I was able to put surgery off as long as I have.

In fact, a year before I actually had my breasts done, I went to see Dr. Giese and she didn't even want to do them.

She said, "You have great breasts. They're better than most women half your age." I've always felt great about my body, but for the last couple of years I felt like my breasts weren't as perky as they used to be. Now that I'm older they had lost some of fullness on top. Some women go crazy and get huge implants, but I didn't want to be bigger. I just wanted to enhance what I already had. I was always a 34 C and I'm still a 34 C. When I went in for my consultation, I put on my Victoria's Secret push up bra, that has a little padding, and I said to Dr. Giese, "This is how I want my breasts to look with a non padded bra. I don't want to have to buy a whole new wardrobe. I want to be able to fit into my clothes. You better not make me any bigger than what I look like right now with this bra on." I wear a size 2 and I didn't want to have to alter all my clothes. I didn't want to be top heavy, I just wanted to be more enhanced. I always had perky boobs; now when I take my bra off I look just as good as I do with it on.

Dr. Giese has a machine in her office that creates before and after images, so I was able to be very specific about what I wanted as well as see what the end result would look like. There are several different kinds of implants; some are contoured to mimic the natural shape of the breast and some are textured to encourage scar tissue to form and prevent repositioning. I chose saline implants because I felt they were more natural, but that's just my preference. The surgeons can go in through the armpit or even the nipple, but I didn't want to do that because it requires a longer recovery period. Dr. Giese put my implants in from underneath the breast; the incision is in the fold. It was a fairly quick procedure and I went home that day. The next day I was a little swollen, and I had to wear a bra that didn't have any wire, but basically I felt fine. I took some Motrin and was actually able to go out to lunch with a friend.

I could go on and on about the alternatives to plastic surgery and the importance of keeping your body and skin healthy, but the truth is that getting my breasts done was the right choice for me when the time came. The most important thing is that you feel as healthy on the inside as you look on the outside.

• 6 •

Game, Set, Match

IT'S MAY OF 2010. I am sitting on a luxurious private jet with nine other women from New York City and California. We are not traveling to a posh resort in St. Tropez or the Cannes Film Festival in France. Not even close. I am in Africa—yes, that's right, Africa—and we are flying to a rural airstrip in the middle of the South African wilderness. For the next sixteen days, we will be visiting four different African countries as we embark on a charitable safari, to raise money for schools in impoverished communities. And, get this, I only have one bag packed. It weighs less than twenty-five pounds and contains little more than three pairs of khaki pants, two pairs of khaki shorts, and six T-shirts.

I am both nervous and exhilarated. I've never been away from my husband and daughter for such a long time. Sure, Avery and I have gone out to Southampton or Aspen a day or so before Mario and Avery has gone away to camp, but I have never been away from both of them for this long or this far away.

I adjust my seat, put on my face mask, close my eyes, and brace myself for the journey of a lifetime.

ONE YEAR EARLIER I had I run into an acquaintance of mine, Krista Krieger, at a social event in Southampton. Krista is the Chairwoman of Empowers Africa, a non-profit organization that works to fund programs that empower rural communities near conservation areas in sub-Saharan Africa. After some small talk, she began telling me about her charity and suggested that I get involved. She explained, "Every spring, I take a group of women to Africa on a wilderness safari and along the way we visit the schools and communities for which we have raised money. I usually bring about six to eight women. You should join us next year."

I stared at her in disbelief. I didn't know anything about her charity. Maybe she had me confused with someone else. Ramona . . . in Africa . . . on a safari . . . a *wilderness* safari? I am not the outdoorsy type. I wear six-inch high heels and designer dresses. When I travel, I fly first class and stay in four-star, luxury hotels. This trip was way out of my comfort zone. I told Krista I was flattered that she was inviting me, but I what I really thought was *there is no way I am going to Africa!*

Just to be polite, I asked, "What does the trip entail?"

"We travel through the African wilderness for about two weeks and visit about five different villages and game reserves. We meet with local communities and check on the progress of the different projects we have funded. It's a magical experience."

"Wow," I said through a tense smile, "that sounds very interesting. Let me think about it. In the meantime, please send me some more details."

"Will do," she responded cheerfully. "Again, I would love it if you could join us."

Although my initial, knee-jerk reaction was to dismiss the idea as something I would never do, the longer I thought about it the more I realized that this was the old Ramona thinking. I reminded myself that this was my year of renewal and part of that process was opening myself up to new challenges and new experiences. The new Ramona was intrigued and up for the challenge.

A few weeks later, I met Krista at the Meadow Club in Southampton. Over dinner, we talked about the trip to Africa and the goals and initiatives of her organization.

"So, Krista, tell me a bit about this trip," I said.

She begins with what feels like a rehearsed speech, "In our sixteen years of operation, we have raised more than $6 million to fund community development projects, in areas of education and healthcare, in six African countries. So far, we have successfully built over 140 classrooms and funded the training of more than five hundred teachers. And, as a result of our donations and initiatives, schools have received government-funded teachers, classroom overcrowding has been reduced, student attendance has increased, and overall learning conditions have improved."

Good grief, I felt like I was in a business meeting. I

always get a hoot out of people who present themselves so formally, especially when I know them socially. Sensing that she was losing my attention, she took a large gulp of wine and changed her tack.

"You will be shocked. The living conditions are dire. The schooling is poor. Children are taught by community elders who may or may not have any formal education or training. Many classrooms are actually located under a shady tree in the hot African sun and have no supplies—no chalkboards, notepads, or pens. They have no kitchens, so they cook in big pots over open fires."

Finally she was speaking to my heart. "Oh my goodness," I said, "that sounds horrible."

She reached into her slim Louis Vuitton handbag and pulled out a bunch of colorful photographs and brochures and placed them on the square table, "Our program raises money to build *real* schools—schools with walls, kitchens, administrative supplies, and student supplies. And after the school is built, the government provides certified teachers so the children learn from trained educators."

As she spoke I looked through the photos. There were images of malnourished children, with round, swollen bellies standing in makeshift classrooms with dirt floors. Then, I saw pictures of smiling children in their newly built classrooms. The joyful expression on their faces brought a tear to my eye. I was touched. I had goose bumps. I felt motivated to act, to get involved immediately. This was a cause and charity where I could make an immediate difference in a child's life.

"Krista, say no more. I'm in."

She looked shocked, "Really?"

"Yes. Tell me what I have to do next."

Over the next few months after that meeting, I prepared for my African safari. I received numerous immunization shots, more than you can possibly imagine—measles, mumps, rubella tetanus, yellow fever, polio, and diphtheria. I also began working to raise money for the charity. On my birthday, I invited forty of my closest friends to my party at the French bistro Chat Noir, an elegant restaurant located in a townhouse on the Upper East Side. The invitation read, *In lieu of gifts, please send donations to the Sanctuary or Empowers Africa. The money we raise will be used to build schools in Africa.*

I was originally supposed to go to Africa with my good friend, Marla. It was comforting to think that I would have her with me, but she had to drop out at the last minute so I ended up going on my own with Krista and eight other women, five of whom I have never even met before. The day before I left I was a nervous wreck. I told everyone I ran into—the doorman of my building, the waiter at Tiramisu, and the owner of our local stationary store—how excited and nervous I was about the trip.

On May 7, 2010, I flew KLM Royal Dutch airlines from JFK to Amsterdam, where my connecting flight was delayed for four hours because of a volcano eruption in Iceland the month before. I finally arrived in Johannesburg close to midnight, twenty grueling hours later, and collapsed into an exhausted sleep in my hotel around 2:00 a.m. The plan was to meet up with the other women early the next morning and fly a charter plane to Kruger National Park, the first stop on our safari. I had set a wake-up call for 8:00 a.m. but that call never came and I woke up from a jet-lagged sleep at 8:30 a.m. All I could think as I rushed to get ready was, *what will these women think of me?* I was meeting most of them for the first time and here I was showing up late on the very first day of our trip. I was so mortified that I asked the concierge for a note, like I was a child who was late for school. Thankfully, the camp liaison covered for me and said it was his fault that I was late so I was able to relax.

After brief introductions, our group loaded into a very small ten-seat private charter plane, the only type of craft compact enough to land on the rural airstrips in the remote locations we would be visiting. An hour later we were deposited onto a solitary strip of tarmac. On either side was an endless expanse of flat scrubby terrain. We were met by two drivers in open-top jeeps and, as we began making our way to camp, along a very narrow dirt road in the African wilderness, all my anxieties of the days leading up to the trip unexpectedly began to fade away. I inhaled deeply. The air in South Africa is invigorating. It has such a clean, pure smell. I knew in that moment I had made the right decision to come and that this experience would change me forever. All the women were so friendly and supportive. No one had an agenda. They were all secure and happy within themselves. It was so different from my experiences traveling on the show.

When we arrived at Ngala Tented Camp, we were greeted by cheerful staff who sang to us while they handed out moist towelettes and a refreshing drink. After we settled in, we had just enough time to unpack and have a quick lunch before heading out for an evening safari. At four o'clock we divided into two groups and set out in two open-air jeeps through Kruger National Park, one of the largest game reserves in Africa. Since this was my first ever safari and I had no idea what to expect, I was both exhilarated and nervous. I wondered how close the animals would come to the jeep. *Are they dangerous? Will I be frightened? Will we see anything good?* Nothing could have prepared me for what we were about to see. The experience exceeded my wildest expectations.

Almost immediately, we had our first sighting—a male leopard, whose stomach was visibly full from a recent kill. We were so close to him that you could see the rise and fall of his chest as he relaxed and digested his meal. We later saw the remains of his kill hanging from a tree, which is how leopards protect their food from scavengers. Not fifteen minutes later we spotted a female leopard hiding in the grass. She was so regal and beautiful. I'm told most people don't get to see leopards on their first safari trip, but here I was, my first day out, and I was lucky enough to see not just one, but two of the majestic creatures. Along with lions, elephants, black and white rhinos, and Cape buffalo, leopards are considered one of the big five game, a term safari guides use to describe the top five most difficult animals to spot. I felt truly blessed. Over the course of the trip we went on to see all of the big five game, as well as giraffes, zebras, elephants, hippos, and impalas—which are as common there as deer in Southampton.

When the sun had set, we pulled over and our spotter and guide set up tables with lanterns for cocktails under the brilliant African night sky. These were the brightest stars I have ever seen and the sheer number of them is almost impossible to comprehend. There are constellations like the Southern Cross and Scorpio constellations that can't be seen from our hemisphere. As we packed up and got ready to head back to camp for dinner, the spotter shone his light to the left and suddenly hundreds of Cape buffalo were illuminated barely one hundred meters away from where we were sitting. All I could think was, thank goodness they hadn't decided to come our way or we would have been stampeded. We piled back into the jeeps and headed back to camp. Just as we were beginning to process the marvel of the herd of Cape buffalo, we encountered a parade of enormous elephants crossing the road ahead of us. We had to pull over and wait for them to pass through. Seeing these enormous creatures in person I finally understood the phrase "hung like an elephant"—it truly looks like a fifth appendage.

The next morning I awoke to the sound of a friendly voice calling out good morning and a tray with a breakfast of oatmeal and fresh fruit outside my door. I felt totally relaxed. For the first time in my life I wasn't worried about anything; not my businesses, not taking care of my two homes, not even my family. It was so liberating. I took the breakfast out to my terrace and the mango was so sweet and delicious it was like I was tasting it for the first time. Even though I had heard stories about monkeys invading the outdoor showers, I decided to risk it and bathe al fresco.

That day we drove out to visit the local preschool, primary, and high school. The highlight of the day was when we visited Mahlale High School and got to see the kitchen they were building with the money we had raised leading up to the trip. Not only do the schools serve lunch and cook on the premises, they actually grow all their own vegetables. The children tend the gardens and pick the vegetables for their meals. For most of these children, many of whom walk miles from home, their only meal of the day is at this school. What really impressed me the most were the smiles on every child's face. They have the brightest smiles you have ever

Welverdiend Primary School, South Africa

seen. These children have few material possessions, yet they were beaming with happiness. It put into perspective for me how materialistic we are in the West.

The next stop on our trip was the Okavango Delta in Botswana, which reminded me a bit of the Florida Everglades. The grass is high and endless and water lilies are everywhere you look. I must have seen a thousand different shades of green. After settling into our rooms at Xaranna Camp, we took a boat to get to a dry area of land where we could see game. To navigate the delta, you have to ride in a makoro boat, which is a type of canoe that is propelled by standing on the stern and pushing with a pole. On our first full day at Xaranna Camp, I wrote in my journal:

> Woke up leisurely and saw the sunrise from my bed. So breathtaking. Took my outdoor shower and felt one with my surroundings. This a.m., did a mokoro boat ride. It's very low in the water and smooth as glass. As we cut through delicate three-foot tall reeds, I felt as if I was gliding on top of the water. So many water lilies, to the left and right, like a floral carpet on the water. The giraffe are so quiet you don't even feel their presence until they are already upon you. It was all so surreal. I felt relaxed and spiritually connected to the world around me.

The second camp we stayed at in Botswana, Mombo Camp, was elevated on stilts. The guest rooms and connecting walkways were all six feet off the ground, which allows game to wander freely beneath the camp. After sunset we

Mombo Camp, Botswana

had to be escorted to our rooms, so no room hopping in the evenings at Mombo. One of the women in our group was awakened in the middle of the night by an elephant under her room. The next night she slept in her clothes in case she had to make a run for it. One week into the trip, the only game in the big five we had not seen, other than the rhino, was the lion. In Botswana we encountered an entire pride. We spotted their tracks and then came upon them, lying in the shade with four cubs sleeping one on top of the other. Later that same day, in the same spot, we saw four lionesses cruising with their cubs and we got to see the cubs rolling

Victoria Falls, the smoke that thunders

around and being frisky. We watched in amazement as the lionesses fell into formation to hunt and kill an impala. Almost as remarkable as the lions, we saw monkeys with large round testicles of the brightest blue you can possibly imagine, which gave new meaning to the term "blue balls." On our last morning at Mombo Camp, while I was eating breakfast on my deck, I watched two elephants stroll by as casually as commuters on their way to work.

The last leg of our trip was through Zambia and Namibia. In Zambia, our pilot flew over Victoria Falls before we landed. One of the Seven Wonders of the World, the enormity of this waterfall is mind-blowing. It's a mile wide and twice as high as Niagara Falls. As we approached the falls, the air appeared to be filled with endless smoke, but as we flew closer we realized that it was actually the vapor and spray released by the cascading water. The indigenous name of Victoria Falls, Mosi-oa-Tunya, actually means "the smoke that thunders." From the air you can see a rainbow spanning the side of the falls. After we landed, we were taken by bus for a closer tour. Our guide handed out ponchos because the spray coming off the falls is so powerful it feels like a monsoon. There were moments when the force of the water coming at me was so strong that I had to turn my face away from the falls.

Our camp in Zambia, Toka Leya Tented Camp, was built under a shady canopy of jackalberry and waterberry trees along the Zambezi River, the fourth largest river system in Africa. That night we took a sunset cruise, where I saw hippos up close for the first time. We also saw crocodiles. This was not like seeing them in a zoo; they are so well camouflaged in the water that you don't see them until they are almost upon you. At one point, I was sitting on the bow edge at the front of the boat and a crocodile appeared out of nowhere, silently slicing through the lily pads on the surface of the still water, and heading straight toward me. I screamed and nearly jumped out of my skin.

Every country we visited had different topography and was a unique visual experience. Namibia was no exception. The landscape was unlike anything we had seen yet. There wasn't a single green bush or tree. Everything was dry. It is called the Sand Sea, because of its towering dunes of fine, rust colored sand. I have never felt anything like the texture of this sand. It is a brilliant orange but leaves no residue on your skin. We camped at Little Kulala, a beautiful lodge with bleached white floors, white walls, and white couches. It had a communal area with a wine cellar that you had to step down into, like a hidden cave full of twinkling candles.

By this point, I had bonded with the nine other women I had been traveling with. We had a camaraderie, respect, and positive energy. There was not one single argument the entire trip, a far cry from my trips with the ladies on the show. I wanted to do something special to show my appreciation, so I decided to host a cocktail party in the camp's wine cellar on our last night there. I had the staff deliver handwritten letters to each of the women, inviting them to join me that evening. Beneath a backdrop of hundreds of candles flickering against the deep dark walls of the cellar, I raised a glass and toasted my new friends. I thanked them for embracing me with open arms and allowing me to open myself up to this life-changing experience. I actually started to choke up and get tears in my eyes. I felt so blessed to be in the midst of nine other secure, giving, and successful women.

The final stop on our trip was Desert Rhino Camp in Damaraland, home of the rare, desert-adapted black rhino, where we presented four hippo rollers to the local community. These devices, which consist of long handles attached to barrel-shaped containers, transport water more easily and efficiently than the traditional method. They roll along the ground, almost like a handheld lawn mower, so the women of the community no longer have to carry heavy drums of water on their heads. They can carry up to ninety liters of water and are so easy to fill and transport that even young children and old women can use them.

We were also in Damaraland to track the black rhino. We took jeeps out and the trackers went on ahead of us. When we got a radio call that the rhino had been spotted, we set out after them on foot. We walked a mile along rugged terrain of large broken rocks. It would have been easy to lose your footing, so we had to look down at our feet and sometimes hold hands to keep from losing balance. Finally we spotted them, two black rhinos just a hundred meters away. Luckily we were upwind so they didn't catch our scent and charge after us.

That was my last day in Africa and it was exhilarating to have both spotted the black rhino and see that we had a positive impact on the local community. I never thought I would survive one day, much less sixteen, with a group of women I had never met before, on a continent half a world away from home. That night we watched the sunset together, drank wine, and laughed like old friends. Two years earlier, I would have never considered going on this trip—never considered leaving my family—but I was a new, renewed Ramona. I had opened myself up to the challenge and was rewarded tenfold. The trip turned out to be a life-changing experience. Something out of my element, my realm, my comfort zone. Something spiritual. Something special.

I have always been involved in local and national charities. I have done behind-the-scenes activities and assisted in fundraising initiatives. But this was different. This was a hands-on experience halfway across the world. I actually saw—with my own eyes—where the money we raised was going and used my own two hands to help improve the lives of the women and children in the communities we had visited.

As shortsighted as it may sound, prior to this experience, when it came to helping children I always thought I should focus on charities at home in the U.S. Yet, as I evolved and renewed myself, I began to realize that the only way to help other nations emerge from poverty is through the education and preservation of its children. Without education, they will always remain behind. I was grateful to have had the chance to make a direct impact on the lives of people in several African communities.

My journey through Africa was a spiritual experience that opened my eyes to the world. All the women I traveled with had gotten along; there was no arguing and no drama. I came back to New York feeling so peaceful and rejuvenated. Unfortunately, my newfound sense of tranquility was short-lived. A few days after I returned, we filmed the Reunion episode for Season 3 and I felt as if I had been thrown back into the lion's den—and that's after being in the wild with actual lions. Reunions are always very intense and stressful, but this time I was determined to maintain my new Zen-like attitude. In fact, I remember Andy Cohen saying he couldn't believe how calm I was. I said, "Hey, I just came back from Africa."

I even did my best to diffuse the tension between Bethenny and Kelly. At one point I got upset because I felt like Kelly wouldn't stop ranting about Bethenny's PR people attacking her on *Page 6*, which I don't believe is true. I didn't want to say, "Shut up, Kelly," so instead I stood up and said, "Oh, I'm so hot," and started walking around, flipping the skirt of my dress. They all thought I as was having a hot flash, but I was actually just trying to interrupt Kelly. The only time I got *Ramotional* was when I got up in front of Jill and stamped my feet because I was so upset about how she had treated Bethenny and how she had showed up at the villa in St. John. I felt she owed all of us an apology for how she had handled things that season.

The next season was even harder. I felt Jill was controlling everything that Kelly and Cindy were doing, that they became their own separate clique and weren't thinking independently. I also felt that Jill was bitter about Bethenny and that she was taking all of her frustrations and anger out on me. By the end of that season I was miserable and began to focus more and more on my businesses as a way to avoid my feelings. After that Reunion, I remember one of the producers asking me how I would feel about filming with Jill for Season 5. I told her, "Somehow I'll make it work. I don't know how, but I always make it work. I'll figure it out." I remember her saying to me, "Ramona, that's what we like about you, you're a team player." So I was completely shocked when I found that Jill, Alex, Cindy, and Kelly weren't coming back for the upcoming season. I couldn't believe that Bravo had the balls to get rid of half the cast, but I figured the producers must know what they were doing.

After all the tension and negative energy I experienced during the filming of Season 4, I was looking forward to working with a new group of women for Season 5. LuAnn, Sonja and I were joined by three new women: Heather Thomson, Carole Radziwill, and Aviva Drescher. There's a moment at the end of the first episode of that season when you see the three new ladies at lunch together for the first time, Aviva says to Carole and Heather, "I don't want us to become mean girls," and Heather replies, "No, never." Unfortunately, I didn't feel that they kept their promise to one another and I ended up butting heads with both of these women over the course of that season.

Right away, Heather rubbed me the wrong way. I remember her saying to me early on that the cameras weren't going to catch *her* doing anything wrong. To me, that comment did not seem genuine and after my experience with the women on my trip to Africa, it was important to me that I surround myself with genuine people. My other issue with Heather was that you could see in her eyes when she was getting angry, but she would smile as though she wasn't. I said to her, "Your eyes aren't matching your smile." I may not always say the right thing, but I am always true to who I am. Then Heather invited all the other women on the show to join her in London except me. I was hurt that she didn't invite me, partly because it did not feel good to be excluded, but also because I felt like she was acting like she hadn't done it intentionally to hurt my feelings when it seemed obvious to me that she had. At that point, I considered her a phony and a fake.

Heather and I were in conflict almost that entire season. She was helping Sonja with her toaster oven campaign, and it seemed that Sonja was getting frustrated because her point of view wasn't being heard. Heather wanted Sonja to put the muscular torso of a man on the box and I thought, *who wants to buy a toaster oven from a half-naked man?* If I'm a housewife or a grandmother, I'm going to buy a toaster oven because Sonja Morgan is on the box, not some random naked guy. I loved Sonja's idea to have herself,

Season 7, Turks and Caicos

looking glamorous and beautiful, on the box, but I think she didn't speak up because Heather can be very intimidating. I ended up repeatedly speaking up on Sonja's behalf, which was a mistake. By the end of the season, I finally realized I needed to stop fighting Sonja's battles because it was only making my relationship with Heather worse.

Thankfully, Carole and I hit it off immediately. She has a wonderful free spirit and true depth of character. I have tremendous respect for her as an accomplished producer, journalist, and author. We're very different; she's very downtown and I'm very uptown, but we've always gotten along very well. In fact, my friendship with Carole has definitely influenced me because my look is becoming much more downtown. I'm not always wearing those proper dresses and heels that I used to live in. I've loosened up and my look has become more edgy.

The biggest surprise for me was how I wound up falling out with Aviva over the course of Season 5. Initially we got along well, but then it seemed as if she just turned 180 degrees on me. The tension between us began even before all the drama in St. Barts, but it skyrocketed to a whole new level after that. My experience with Aviva has been that if you don't do what she wants you to do, she gets very angry and spiteful. When I questioned why she had brought her husband on our girls' vacation to St. Barts, she got furious. I do feel that LuAnn stirred the pot by telling her that we had joked about asking Reid to stay at a hotel. I don't know why she repeated that. Maybe she wanted to redirect the focus away from us questioning her about Tomas, the Johnny-Depp-in-*Pirates of the Caribbean*-look-alike we met at the nightclub, Le Ti. During the Reunion episode LuAnn admitted to bringing him back to the house, but denied that anything physical happened between them. All I know is, LuAnn loves men and men love LuAnn, so I can only begin to imagine what really happened. I do think that if she *was* trying to deflect attention, it was a very smart strategy on her part

Photo on the wall at Le Ti

because once Aviva called Sonja and me "white trash" no one was thinking about LuAnn and the pirate anymore. After that, I felt like Aviva went crazy on Sonja and me. Sonja rarely loses her temper. Generally, she takes on a very calming role when there is a conflict, but this fight even pushed her buttons. My favorite line of that season was when she took back her apology to Aviva and said, "Can I get a Return to Sender?"

One of the most intense moments of that season for me was when I met Aviva for tea after we got back from St. Barts. After I shot that scene with her, I felt bruised as though she had punched me with her words. I had already apologized several times and sincerely hoped that at this meeting would enable us to get to a better place. Harry, Aviva's ex-husband, and I have been friends for years, long before I met Aviva. I had called him to see if he could give me some insight into why Aviva had gotten so angry. Unfortunately, she mistook my concern as criticism of her phobias. I honestly did want to mend fences with Aviva. I know I am not perfect and I too can overreact in stressful situations. I did not want the conflict to continue. Life is too short to hold onto ill will and anger for extended periods of time. That's why I could not believe the anger that I felt was being directed at me at that day. At times, it seemed even more intense than anger; I felt there was hatred in her eyes. It was as if Aviva became a snake full of venom and vile words. Part of me was in shock. For a while I was frozen in my chair and then I just had enough. When I get upset, I'm the type of person who can't deal with someone getting angry with me so I tend to walk away. I admit that's not always a good trait, but this time I really just couldn't take anymore. I remember that afterwards the head producer said that he couldn't believe how long I sat there and I replied, "Well, you always tell me I end the conversation too quickly when I get upset and I run away, so I thought I'd make you happy."

Other than showing up in St. Barts with her husband in tow, Aviva always seemed to have a reason not to join us on our trips. She'd say it was her phobias or asthma, but I believe that the real reason is that she does not want to push herself out of her comfort zone. I think that when she's backed into a corner or her motives are questioned, she feels the need to create drama the way she did in the final episode of Season 6 when, at Sonja's party, she slammed her prosthetic leg on the table and then threw it across the room. I believe Aviva did that because she knew she had made a major mistake not coming with us on the trip to Montana and I think she felt that she needed to do something to redeem herself. In my opinion, it was a very calculated move. Our show is completely real and unscripted, which is why it has been so successful, but I believe that Aviva had scripted that scene in her head long before she got to the party. I've seen her remove her prosthetic and it takes deliberation, so I don't see how in the heat of the moment she could have had the presence of mind to unbuckle it that quickly and whip it onto the table.

All of a sudden, BOOM, there was a leg on the table. We were all shocked, so I do think she got the reaction she wanted. Every jaw in the room dropped. You almost felt like she had cut off her leg because her prosthetic is so realistic looking. I remember Kristen Taekman, who was new to the show that season, blurted out that she felt like she was going to vomit. People were offended by that comment, but I understood where she was coming from. Aviva's leg is very lifelike so having it suddenly appear on the table was like something out of a horror movie. I remember, in Season 5, Reid played a practical joke on me using Aviva's prosthetic. We were at their home in Miami and they had Mario and me stay in their gorgeous master bedroom. I was in the huge walk-in closet and when I walked back into the room, one of Aviva's prosthetic legs was on the side table. I freaked out for a second because I thought someone had been murdered and dismembered. It was a very jarring experience.

Although I've had my differences with Aviva, we have moved on from that confrontation and we are still friends.

The Singers on safari in Africa

I was actually having lunch with her recently when Andy Cohen called to thank me for being so open about my life during the filming of Season 7. (That was a little awkward.) I think Aviva needs to feel in control and she has a hard time putting herself in a situation where that might not be the case. I understand that impulse. It's the reason that I was initially reluctant to go to Africa. There were too many unknowns, I would have to rely on other people, and I wouldn't have any control. But I took a leap of faith and it wound up being the most exhilarating and spiritual experience of my life.

In 2013, I returned to South Africa with Avery and

Mario. After hearing all about my trip, Avery had been dreaming of seeing Africa for herself and I wanted to share the experience with her. She had been accepted to Emory and would be leaving for college in August, so Mario and I decided to take her to South Africa in April of her senior year as a graduation present.

Our first stop was at Phinda Forest Lodge, in KwaZulu-Natal, a province in southeastern South Africa. Every morning, we got up early for a three-hour safari ride through Phinda Private Game Reserve, so I was able to share with Mario and Avery the wonders of the African wilderness that I had experienced on my first trip. We also visited several schools and a health facility supported by Empowers Africa. At Phinda we visited the first school in this area for handicapped children. Before this school was built, many children who were confined to wheelchairs or had learning or physical disabilities would just stay home alone all day.

Krista Krieger had graciously set up this school visit for us, but we ended up being such a large group that, although it was a beautiful experience, Avery wasn't able to interact with the children as much as she had hoped. She said to me, "Mommy, I really want to have a more intimate experience." So at our next stop, Dulini Lodge in Sabi Sands Game Reserve near Kruger National Park, we went to another school and had a much more hands-on experience. We had learned that the boys play soccer and the girls play a game called netball, which is similar to basketball, so we bought and donated sports equipment to the school (soccer balls for the boys and netball hoops for the girls). One of

Avery with school children in South Africa

the best moments of the trip was when they gave Avery a uniform to wear and she got to play netball with the girls at the school.

We had already started filming for Season 6 by then, but I took the time off because I felt it was important for Mario, Avery, and I to have that time together as a family before she left for college. That trip was an incredible bonding experience for us. I wanted to teach my daughter the valuable lesson that I had learned on my own trip three years earlier. To truly grow as a person you have to take yourself out of your element and open yourself up to change and new experiences.

Little did I know, however, that I was about to be taken forever out of my comfort zone. Over the following year, my marriage of twenty-one years collapsed in an excruciatingly public way, and I found myself sorting through the rubble of my life in search of some kind of foundation upon which to begin rebuilding.

Our first wedding day, March 1992

• 7 •

What Happened To Happily Ever After?

I AM STANDING IN THE master bedroom of a magnificent two-bedroom suite at the Pierre Hotel in New York City. I stare at the one-inch thick deck of index cards in my hands and begin practicing my marital vows. *I can't believe I am marrying Mario*, I say to myself. *Today is going to be one of the happiest days of my life*. Like any bride on her wedding day, I am nervous and apprehensive. I have butterflies in my stomach and goose bumps on my arms. I'm worried about how I will look in my dress and whether the groom will be on time.

Actually, although I still consider myself young (thank you very much), I'm not exactly a blushing bride. It's December 16, 2009 and I am about to marry my husband—for the second time. We haven't been separated or divorced; we are reaffirming our commitment and loyalty to one another by renewing our vows. Our first wedding day, almost eighteen years ago, was in March of 1992, but today I feel as if I am marrying Mario for the very first time.

A few months ago, I approached him with this idea of a vow renewal ceremony. I could have waited for a milestone anniversary, but the timing felt right. I was renewing other aspects of my life so why not renew one of the most important: my marriage and my relationship with my husband? And, since I never do anything on a small scale, I wanted Mario and I to stand in front of our daughter and closest friends—just a few cameramen and over a million *Real Housewives of New York City* viewers—and profess our love and loyalty to one another. Being the loving, supportive husband that he is, Mario agreed. (Okay, maybe the sexy, black lingerie I was wearing and the glass of bubbly champagne he was drinking when I proposed the idea may have persuaded him a bit, but never mind.)

My newly short blonde hair has been trimmed and blown out by my hairstylist, Oscar Blandi, and I slip into my gorgeous Kimberly Towers wedding dress. It's a stunning strapless gown made of ivory duchess silk satin, with a ruched, form-fitting bodice and whimsical ostrich feathers and crystals on the bottom skirt. When I look at myself in the six-foot, Venetian, tri-fold mirror, I truly feel like a bride on her wedding day. I am one hundred percent confident that I made the right decision to marry Mario. I can't say I felt that way on our first wedding day. I knew that I loved Mario, but I was so scarred by my parents' dysfunctional relationship that I had no faith in the unity of marriage. I saw marriage as a prison and had a history of choosing emotionally distant men as a way to avoid becoming trapped. When

I decided to marry Mario, I took a leap of faith that our relationship would be based on mutual love and respect and, for nearly eighteen years, that is exactly what our marriage has been.

My thoughts are suddenly interrupted when a vision of my younger self appears in the mirror by my side. For a split second I think I am hallucinating, but then I realize Avery is standing beside me. She is wearing a royal blue silk satin dress trimmed with silver and periwinkle rhinestones. She slips on her Badgley Mischka sequined heels and asks me to fasten the clasp of her necklace, which I have given her from my jewelry collection. My eyes begin to swell with tears. This moment is surreal. For the very first time, I am seeing my daughter as the graceful young woman she is poised to become. It is as if I am seeing her from an entirely new vantage point. I think to myself, *I can't believe how quickly Avery has grown up. Mario and I are so blessed to have her in our lives.*

I take Avery's hand and we walk to The Rotunda, the Pierre's signature room, where the ceremony is being held. It is a beautiful, elegant cream-colored room, with hand-painted frescos on the high ceiling. I see Mario. He is wearing a black tuxedo and is as handsome as ever. He is pacing back and forth, reciting his vows.

"Mario, are you okay?" I ask. "You look nervous."

Before he can respond, Avery interjects, "What's wrong with you two? Why are you so nervous? You're already married!"

"That's true, honey," Mario says, "but the last time we got married, we weren't doing it in front of millions of viewers who will blog about the ceremony and point out every little mistake we make."

I laugh. Leave it to Mario to put us all at ease.

Suddenly the instrumental music begins. Mario walks down the baluster staircase on cue. He is followed by Avery, who is carrying our dog, Coco. They are so adorable in their matching blue dresses. They position themselves at the center of the picturesque, pale yellow rotunda at the center of the base of the stairs.

The music changes and it's my turn to walk down the staircase. I take a deep breath and step carefully, gripping my hand on the golden banister. I am wearing six-inch platform, silver metallic Casadei heels and I don't want to fall . . . especially not on camera. As I descend, I look into the faces of my close friends who have gathered here to support us. I feel so vibrant, beautiful and alive. I turn and face Mario. He has tears in his hazel eyes. At that moment, I can feel the love he has for me. We join hands. All my fears and nerves subside. In this moment, I realize that I love Mario even more today than the day I married him.

Adam, our good friend for many years, begins the ceremony. He says wonderful things about our loving relationship, our equal partnership, and our parenting of Avery. I recite my vows and, at one point, I am so overcome with emotion that my voice cracks and I almost lose it. Then it is Mario's turn:

Ramona,

Probably the biggest decision one will ever make is the person to spend the rest of your life with. Sometimes it takes quite a while before you know if you've made the right choice. I was fortunate to have known very early that I had made the right decision. My mom had suffered a stroke and she would need care for the rest of her life. Since Dad had already passed away I asked you if it was alright if my mom could live with us in our home in Southampton. Not only did you take her in but you embraced her with love and kindness like she was your own mother. That is when I knew I had made the right decision. I had absolutely chosen the women I would spend the rest of my life with. For seventeen years of marriage you have been at my side through everything that life has thrown at us, both good and bad. You have been a steady rock in times of trouble and a ray of sunshine when I could not see the light. You have applauded my achievements and comforted me in my setbacks. You have given me the most wonderful daughter a father could ever have. For all of this I am blessed and so I reaffirm my vows that I said so long ago. Ramona, I will love and honor you through good times and bad for better or worse in sickness and in health until death do us part. May God continue to bless our marriage.

His vows are honest, loving, and heartfelt. We kiss, a slow romantic kiss. I open my eyes and look to my daughter and then out to our friends. There is not a dry eye in the house.

THAT WAS ONE of the happiest moments of my life, second only to the birth of my daughter. If someone had told me on that day that my marriage would be over in four years, and the intimate details of its collapse would become fodder for tabloid headlines, I would never have believed it. Mario and I were so happy for so many years. We were the perfect couple and when Avery came into our lives we became the perfect family. We proudly referred to ourselves as *a trifecta*. We had an impenetrable family bond that nothing could destroy—or so we thought.

How did this happen to us? How did we end up so broken?

The Trifecta

The first indication I had that Mario was unhappy in our marriage was towards the end of September 2012. I think at that point he was beginning to feel neglected because I had been doing the show for five seasons and, when I wasn't filming, I was traveling all over the country doing signings for Ramona Pinot Grigio. I was just beginning to realize that I had stretched myself too thin and had taken my eye off my other businesses. I can see now that I had taken my eye off my marriage as well.

When Mario expressed that he was unhappy it broke my heart because I had no idea that I had been hurting him. I remember he told me that he was unhappy and that he felt like I had been chipping away at him; it bothered him when I rushed him off the tennis court or snapped at him when

we were running late for an event. I promised to stop doing those things, and I kept my promise. We spent that weekend talking, crying, and making mad passionate love over and over again. It was if our bodies had been ignited by opening up to each other.

In December, we took Avery on vacation to Anguilla. Some close friends were renting a villa on the beach near our hotel and Avery would have sleepovers with their daughter, so Mario and I had plenty of romantic time. All the passion and warmth we had been feeling over the last couple of months continued to build. We had a private balcony with a hot tub that was so enormous it was like having a mini pool on our terrace. It was so secluded you could spend your days and nights completely nude and no one could see you. For seven days we made love in the oversized hot tub, worked out together, ate romantic dinners, and walked along the beach. I remember, one evening, swimming together in the infinity pool by the hotel bar, Mario's arms encircling me as we watched the sunset. I felt so complete in that moment and I told Mario how blessed I felt that, after all these years, we still had such an intense connection. With Avery leaving for college, I would have been devastated if we didn't have one another. We celebrated New Year's Eve in Anguilla and, as we moved into 2013, I felt confident things between us were back on track; Mario wrote me a beautiful, meaningful card for Valentine's Day and we celebrated our twenty-first wedding anniversary in March.

I think things started to go downhill when Mario found out how much I was going to make for Season 6 of *Real Housewives*. We began filming in May and it was in June,

At our friend Denise Rich's Christmas party, ca. 1998

while we were away in Africa, that I first noticed him pulling away from me. Even though we were on this amazing family vacation, he seemed distant and out of sync with me. Mario had just turned sixty, Avery was about to leave for college, and his business was struggling. On top of that, his wife of twenty-one years had become famous and was earning a great salary. I think he just wasn't feeling good about himself. Looking back, I think if filming had started in the fall we would have been okay. After we returned from Africa, I was filming seven or eight times a week, sometimes twice a day, and I was preoccupied with Avery leaving for college. I told myself, *at the end of September, I will concentrate on Mario.* Little did I know that by the end of September it would be too late. I had no clue that something was shifting in our marriage. Mario didn't communicate that he was still unhappy and I didn't see the path he was on was leading him further and further away from our marriage.

One day, at the end of August, I remember Mario running out to play tennis at a friend's. He said he was going to shower there and meet me later at a party. I noticed that he had left his wedding ring on the nightstand and I remember wondering, *why isn't he wearing his ring? Should I ask him?* But something held me back and I never called him on it. I couldn't deal with what it could mean, so I convinced myself that it wasn't a big deal. Meanwhile, a friend of Mario's, who had been divorced for years, had become a permanent fixture at our home that summer and I felt like it was infringing on our privacy. I remember his friend would disappear during the day for a bit to give us alone time, but in the evenings he came to all the parties with us and I began to feel that he was encouraging Mario to go to the ones that were more geared toward singles. It seemed to me that this friend, who I didn't think was very attractive and hadn't had a girlfriend in years, was using Mario as bait to meet single girls at these parties and he would take Mario away from me to troll around and flirt. I remember more than once when I went looking for Mario, I found him surrounded by single women. They would be standing very close to him and it seemed like when I approached, they would take a step back. It started to feel like Mario was more interested in going to parties than hanging out with our married friends. Looking back, these things all seem like obvious red flags, but at the time I let it all go because I thought, *what's the harm if my husband is happy?* That was my biggest mistake.

June and July were good, but by August and September I felt Mario's behavior was becoming increasingly erratic. He seemed irritable and angry and I began to worry about his emotional health. He had been having issues with his knee and couldn't play tennis, which was his usual way of releasing stress, so I tried to be patient with him. But, despite my efforts to be sweet and calm, by the end of September I felt like he was becoming more and more confrontational. At one point, one of my close girlfriends witnessed us having a huge blowout and she expressed concern that Mario wasn't treating me well. She also told me that she had noticed that he was gone for forty-five minutes when he took our dog, Coco, out for a walk. She felt this was suspicious and asked me if I thought it was possible he could be having an affair, "When men disappear for long stretches like that to walk the dog, they are usually talking to their girlfriends." At the time I laughed it off because, of course, that wasn't happening to *me*. Mario wasn't being unfaithful. It was inconceivable.

All that summer and into the fall, I was working nonstop. I remember the night of the cast party after we wrapped filming for Season 6, I wanted Mario to come with me like he always had at the end of every other season, but he said he was going to Westchester with a friend instead and didn't come home until after midnight. What can you do in Westchester after midnight? If I questioned where he was, I felt he would get defensive and snap at me. At that point I felt his behavior had become unacceptable so I decided to go to our Southampton house by myself for the weekend to get some space. When I came home, I remember Mario told me he thought he needed to move out for a while. For the first time I considered the possibility that there might be another woman and I asked him straight out if there was.

He told me no and I believed him.

After that, he gave me a letter in which he explained how unhappy he had been. I tried to understand where this was coming from because I felt that we had been happy all summer. I remember his response was that it was because he was a good actor. I told him that we owed it to our marriage to go to counseling, so we started going to therapy together and I was hopeful that we would figure out a way to resolve our issues.

That October, I remember walking along Park Avenue with one of my good friends, before going to therapy one day, and she said to me, "I hate to be the one to tell you this, but I think you need to know," she paused and then said slowly, "I think Mario has been seeing another woman."

"What are you talking about?" I said, in complete denial.

"Well, you know the other night when we were at Plaza Athénée for that party. People overheard him arguing with a woman on his cell phone when he was in the men's room. He was screaming at her."

I was stunned. I remembered that Mario had gone off that night to make a phone call and I had to admit that I did think he was gone for a little too long. I had also thought it was strange that he had wanted to meet me at the party since Mario hates arriving at events on his own. That evening we went to therapy and I decided to bring up what my friend had told me. Although I felt as if we had been making progress and I didn't want him to think I didn't trust him, I couldn't get what she had told me out of my head. I asked him if he had been fighting on the phone with a woman at the Plaza Athénée party, but I felt like he just brushed me off and made a joke of it so I decided to drop the subject.

At home, later that same night, I walked into the den and I saw that Mario was talking on the phone. I remember as soon as I walked into the room he got very stiff.

"Alan, let me go now. Ramona just walked in," he said abruptly and ended the call.

Alan is a good friend, so I said, "Mario, why did you hang up? I would have said hello to Alan."

"This was a different Alan. You don't know him," he answered.

I sat down beside Mario. He seemed to be getting agitated. He asked me why I had come into the room, but I couldn't remember. My mind was blank. Then something in my brain just snapped. It was like a veil had been lifted and it dawned on me that he had not been talking on the phone to a different Alan, or to any man for that matter. I stood up and I looked at him.

"Mario, that wasn't a different Alan on the phone, was it? You were talking to a girl just now, weren't you?"

I remember his face looked like he had seen a ghost. His eyes went wide. His mouth fell open. He had that same expression on his face when I was pregnant with Avery and I told him that my water broke and we had to go the hospital. He looked like a deer in headlights.

"Just admit you were talking to a girl. Just admit it," I shouted.

He snapped out of it and got defensive, "Yes, I was. Do you want to know what else I do with her besides talk?"

Oddly, I suddenly felt calmer than I had in weeks.

I said, "No, that's all I need to know for now," and walked out of the room.

I needed to clear my head so I left the apartment. I met a girlfriend for dinner at a restaurant in the neighborhood and told her what had just happened. When I came back a few hours later, Mario was on the phone with one of our friends and I heard him say, "Ramona just walked in. She's home. She's okay."

At first when I got home he seemed nervous and scared, but an hour or so later he began to seem more and more self-righteous. I remember, we were in our bedroom and Mario asked me if I wanted to know if anything more had happened. I told him he didn't need to say anything because I already knew. I remember he kept saying that it meant nothing and it was just a symptom of his unhappiness. I was in a state of shock and disbelief. How could this be happening? The following morning at breakfast, I remember Mario telling me he was already planning to end it. Famous last (lying) words.

The next day, I was at the gym and I started getting calls from the press saying they were going to come out with an article stating that Mario was seen having dinner with another woman at Serafina. It was like a knife had sliced open my chest, and my guts were ripped from my body. I just kept thinking, *he promised me he wouldn't see her anymore. How could he lie to me like that?* It was bad enough that he was seeing another woman, but now it was going to be in the press that he took her to a restaurant where I am a friend of the owner and my Pinot is served. Why would he disrespect us like that?

I called Mario and said, "A story is coming out that you were seen having dinner with another woman. You didn't see her, did you?"

He said that he had.

I was shocked, "I thought you told me you were going to stop seeing her?"

He said he never told me that.

I thought, *who is this man? How can he tell me at breakfast that he is planning to end it and then turn around the next day and act like we never had that conversation?* I felt like I was losing my mind. It was as if my husband had suddenly become Jekyll and Hyde; one minute he would be warm, loving and remorseful, and the next he would seem defiant, belligerent, and angry. I began to feel like I didn't know which Mario I was going to see from one day to the next. I thought we needed to talk about what was happening in therapy, but Mario seemed reluctant so I agreed to talk over dinner that night. We met at an Italian restaurant downtown. It was such a surreal moment. We were sitting in this beautiful restaurant and my husband was ordering wine as if we were having a normal romantic dinner, but really the bottom had just dropped out of my world.

I said to Mario, "You can't see her anymore. You have to end it."

I remember he looked at me and said, "I can't promise you that."

Basically, I was in shock. *He can't promise me that? What does that mean? Does he think he's going to be with both of us? Who is this man? How can this be happening? This is a nightmare. This isn't real.* In all the years we were married, it never once crossed my mind that my husband would have an affair, much less that it would become a tabloid headline. I remember sitting across the table from Mario and thinking, *this isn't my husband.* I just could not comprehend that this was who he had become. Even now, there's a part of me that thinks of Mario as dead, that the person I sat across from that night was an imposter who invaded his body and took over his mind.

Over the course of the next year, the things that were written in press about Mario and this woman were so much worse than I could ever have imagined that night. It's painful enough to come face to face with the possibility that you have been lied to and betrayed by your partner of twenty-one years, but to have to do that under the harsh, judgmental glare of the tabloid press is humiliating beyond comprehension. I had no time to process what was happening to my marriage, no time to digest the small morsel of truth that I could bear to swallow, before the most horrendous images were being forced down my throat.

At that point, the most important thing to me was to protect Avery. She was already on the edge at school. Not only was she struggling with the transition of being away, she had had a falling out with her best friend from high school, who was also now at college with her, and it was such a small campus that it had impacted all her friendships. She would call me every week crying because it was making her life miserable. The last thing she needed was to be worrying about what was going on with her father and me at home. I was afraid that her knowing about Mario would push her over the edge and I was not going to let that happen. I knew my marriage was already broken, but I wasn't about to take Avery down with us. The morning that the article came out she woke up at 8:00 a.m. to eight missed calls on her cell phone from numbers she didn't recognize. She called us in a panic because she thought someone had died. The one thing Mario and I agreed on at that point was that we needed to keep Avery out of what was going on between us, so we pretended that the article was no big deal. I basically ate crow to protect my daughter. I remember the three of us were on the phone and Mario and I told her it was just the press looking for a comment on a silly article and she shouldn't worry about it. She believed us because she had put her father on a pedestal her entire life. It killed me to lie to Avery like that, but at the time I felt it was the right thing to do.

A week later we went down to Atlanta to visit Avery for Parents Day. I had told Mario at dinner that night that I didn't think he should come with me, but Avery is his daughter too and I think he felt like I was being unfair. So I said, "Alright, Mario. We're going to Atlanta next week. You have to make a decision; you either end it with this girl or you move out. It's your choice, one or the other. When we go to Atlanta I will know if you're texting this girl. I will feel it and I won't be able to hide it from Avery. We're away for four days, do not speak to her and do not text her. We don't want Avery to know anything is going on, so please just don't." Of course, when we went down to Atlanta I was on edge the entire time. I remember shopping with Avery at Sephora and asking her, "Where's your father?" because I sensed that he was off somewhere talking on the phone. If we were at a restaurant and he got up to walk Coco, I would tell him to leave his phone at the table because I could feel that he had been texting her.

At dinner that night, Avery was using my phone and she came across the story that had been in the press. Up to that point she had been living in a bubble at school and hadn't really read the article. I knew I needed to do some damage control, so when she got up from the table I followed her. I cornered her in the bathroom and Avery said to me, "What's going on? You're acting so weird, making Daddy leave his phone at the table. Daddy's all quiet and spacey. I saw that article on your phone, what does it mean?"

I wanted to gauge her state of mind without saying anything that would influence her thinking, so I said, "Avery, what do *you* think of all this? Do *you* think Dad had an affair?"

Without hesitation, she answered, "Obviously, it's ridiculous. That would *never* happen. You and Daddy have one of the best marriages I have ever seen, out of all your friends and my friends' parents. Daddy would never have an affair. You would never have an affair."

I felt my best shot at getting through to Mario at that point was if he heard how unconditionally our daughter trusted us, how much she believed in our marriage, so I said to her, "Okay, when we go back out there, I want you to tell your father that."

When we sat back down at the table, she said to Mario, "Daddy, I saw the article. I'm so sorry. I can't believe people are attacking you like this. You and Mommy have the best marriage. If I had to choose which one of you would have an affair, literally, gun to my head, I couldn't choose. I know you both love each other too much to do something like that."

I hoped that if Mario heard Avery saying that the father she knew would never do that to her mother, it would resonate with him. I felt that his behavior had been so far off from the man that I knew, he must be having some kind of midlife crisis. I truly believed that if he looked into his daughter's eyes and saw how much he had to lose, his love for her would put him back on the right track. I think she did get through to him, because when we got back home we went back into therapy and attempted to resume our normal lives. I even threw a dinner party for twelve at our house in Southampton.

For a little while, things seemed to be getting back to normal. In November, Mario took me to Charleston. He bought me a Chanel bag for my birthday and we had a beautiful time. But, just two weeks later, things seemed to shift again and I began to feel Mario pulling away. It was like Jekyll and Hyde again. I remember our therapist said to me, "Ramona, it's like he's bludgeoning you for whatever he thinks you did to him in the marriage." In December, right before Avery was about to come home for winter break, we took a trip to Naples because Mario was thinking about retiring and wanted to check out what it would be like to live there. The last thing I wanted to do was sell everything off and move to Florida, but I was trying to be a supportive and loving wife and I hoped it would help salvage our marriage for us to get away together. We did make love that weekend, but he seemed distant and detached. We weren't connecting. Everything felt forced. At one point, we were watching the sun set together and I remember Mario pulled out his phone and took a picture of it. Something about it felt wrong to me, like he wasn't really in that moment with me. I felt a deep longing for the sense of connection I had felt just one year earlier while we were watching the sun setting in Anguilla.

The day after we got home from Naples, I was busy preparing for Avery's arrival home for winter break. I remember being annoyed with Mario because he was late getting home from work. I was in Avery's room, making sure it was all set up for her return, when I started receiving texts from a woman telling me, in crude and explicit language, that she had just *been* with my husband in the apartment he was paying for. The text said that Mario loved me and she couldn't be with him because she knew he loved me. She also forwarded me dozens of screenshots of texts and photos that she claimed Mario had sent to her. Among them was the photo Mario had taken with his phone of that sunset he and I had watched together in Naples. I felt like someone had ripped my heart from my chest. When Mario finally got home, he found me in Avery's room, visibly upset. He asked what was wrong and I told him about the texts. Tears stung my eyes and then began streaming down my face.

At that moment, we heard Avery's voice calling, "Hi, I'm home," as she walked through the front door. I remember Mario saying to me, "Ramona, straighten yourself up fast. Avery's here. We don't want her to know anything." I froze, numb with shock. I knew she must have heard us fighting and I didn't know what to do or say. It must have seemed to Avery like she had stepped into a twilight zone. Instead of being greeted at the door by her loving parents, she walked into this very tense situation. It was literally the very first time in her entire life she had ever heard us fight. Of course, sometimes we would snap or be petty, but it was always little things like, "Mario, you're not ready" or "Ramona, you didn't clean up," but never anything like the scene that she had just walked in on.

My maternal instincts kicked in and I did my best to pull myself together and put on a happy front. I said to myself, *I must protect Avery, no matter what.* I walked out of her bedroom, and Avery was standing in the living room with this look on her face that was equal parts confusion and fear. In the six weeks since she had seen me at the end of October, I had lost fifteen pounds. I was emaciated. She kept asking me, "Mommy, what's wrong, you look like a skeleton?" but there was no way I could tell her what was really was going on.

After that, Mario promised to end it. I felt like he could see how much pain I was in and was truly remorseful. The week after Christmas, the three of us drove out to Southampton, stopping to pick up food from La Parmigiana, our favorite restaurant in town, just like we always had after a long drive in from the city. I kept telling myself, *we are the*

Singers. We are a trifecta. We will get through this and things will be like they always were.

But we would never be the same again.

A few days later, Mario got a voicemail from a woman saying that if he didn't give her money she was going to go to the press. At that point there had been only one article, which had been damaging enough. The last thing we needed while we were trying to salvage our marriage was a full-blown media firestorm. Just the threat of it was so stressful that we got into a huge fight. Avery was in her room on the other end of the house, but she heard us screaming at one another. She told me later that it felt like something out of a movie. She described hearing me yell something like, "What are you going to do? We need to protect Avery," and her father answer, "I don't know. It's your problem, Ramona. Deal with it." She couldn't make out a lot of what we were saying, so she crept down the staircase and stood listening at the bottom. That's when she heard her father say, "Ramona, I am one step away from walking out that door," and me scream back, "Why don't you just go fuck her!"

It kills me to think how painful it must have been for Avery to hear us say those things. She told me later that at that moment, she felt as if her world had shattered into a million jagged little pieces. She snapped and just ran. She ran out the door, into a torrential rainstorm, and collapsed onto the ground. She pulled out her cell phone, and did what any teenage girl would do when she realizes her life is falling apart; she called her best friend. That's when Mario must have heard her outside. Avery was screaming and hysterically crying and, not realizing that she had overheard us arguing, he thought she was in physical pain. He ran out after her into the pouring rain, but when he tried to approach her she screamed, "Don't come near me. You cheated on Mommy. Fuck you. I hate you. Don't come closer. Get away from me." Mario came to get me and eventually we got Avery to calm down enough to come back inside. Later, Avery told me that she had asked Mario not to tell me what she had heard, because she didn't want to upset me, but I think he didn't know what else to do so he told me anyway.

I remember being panicked, thinking, *what do I do? What do I tell her?* I was crying. Avery was crying. It was awful. I couldn't stand seeing my daughter in such pain, so I made a decision to take control of the situation and find a way to convince my daughter that she had misunderstood. I remember the three of us sitting down in our finished basement, where we have this long L-shaped couch. Avery and I were sitting next to one another on one end of the couch and Mario was way over on the far end. I remember looking at him, just sitting there, staring down at the floor, quiet as a mouse. He might as well have been a thousand miles away.

I needed to assess what she thought she knew, so I asked, "Avery, what did you hear?"

"I heard that there's a woman or someone who's threatening us. I heard Daddy say he was one step from walking out the door. And I heard you say something like, 'why don't you go fuck her.'"

The most convincing lies are steeped in truth, so I very delicately spun a web using threads of what she had heard and what I knew she wanted to believe.

"Avery, you misunderstood what we were saying. There is a woman who is *stalking* your father. She wants our money. She's the one who published the fake article in the press. When I said, 'Go fuck her,' I didn't mean physically. I meant, 'Screw her. Who cares what she does? She can't hurt us.'"

I looked into my daughter's eyes and what I saw there in that moment was pure relief. Avery is not a naive person. She is a very intelligent and savvy young woman who can smell bullshit from a mile away. She believed my lie because for most of her life, we were the perfect family. We raised her with a very strong sense of morality. She idolized her father. Mario was always a moral, Christian, god-fearing man. Every Sunday, until she was thirteen years old, he dragged her out of bed to go to church. It was so much easier to believe the lie I told her than what she had heard with her own ears.

Meanwhile, I was deteriorating physically and emotionally. I was disappearing into myself. I couldn't eat. I couldn't sleep. I knew once Avery went back to college, I would be alone with Mario and I was beginning to realize that I couldn't be around him anymore. It felt like no matter what I did, he seemed to be getting angrier and angrier with me. I think he was, in fact, angry with himself for being unfaithful, but he turned his rage on me because he couldn't handle the guilt. He never laid a hand on me, but he would get this white rage in his eyes and I began to feel very threatened and afraid. The stress of everything became unmanageable and it began to wreak havoc on my mind, body, and spirit. There were times when I was so low that I almost felt like throwing myself in front of a subway train. I was so anxious and depressed that my doctor put me on anxiety medication.

I think it was at this point that Mario finally began to see how much of a toll everything we were going through had taken on me. In January, we took Avery to see *Kinky Boots* and I kept nodding off because I was taking too much anxiety medication. I didn't realize it at the time, but I was overmedicating myself to combat depression. I remember Mario taking my hand to nudge me awake, and when I looked at him, for the first time I thought I could see a sign that he wanted my forgiveness. But, at that point, I was so emotionally broken that I couldn't find it in myself to forgive. In order to forgive him, I needed to heal and, in order to heal, I needed time on my own, away from Mario. I was so distraught that I was having terrible diarrhea. My stomach was tied up in knots from stress and it had gotten to the point that whenever I was around him I would lose my stool. I had to get my health back on track.

A week or so before Avery went back to college I took her to lunch and asked her how she would feel if I asked her father to move out.

"Why?" she asked, warily.

"Because things are strained among us right now; we need to have a break. Your father is full of anger towards me, as you have witnessed, and I'm nervous around him." She hugged me and said, "Mommy, I support you. I don't really understand, but I support you."

That last week Avery was home, I basically avoided Mario as much as I could. For the first time *I* was the one pulling away and I think Mario felt it. In fact, Avery told me he kept asking her, *have you heard from your mom, where is your mom?* Then one night I came home and Avery told me that Mario had come into her room. He was very distraught, and was questioning her about me in a very intense and aggressive way.

"Daddy's looking for you. He said he needs to talk to you. He kept pushing me to tell him if you had said anything about what's wrong with you. I kept saying that I didn't feel it was my place. I was like, 'Daddy, I don't want to get in the middle of this. All I can say is that Mom's really not okay.' But he kept pushing, 'Your mom is going to ask me to move out, isn't she? Tell me your mom told you she wants me out.' He was freaking out, so I told him you said you were going to ask him to move out after I go back to school. He just broke down and started crying. Dad *never* cries. He was saying, 'I know. I've been awful. I've been pushing her away, Avery, and I think I pushed her too far. I love her so much. I'm sorry. I've done some awful things. I haven't been the man that I was.' He was acting so weird. I said, 'Dad, *did* you have an affair?' He just kind of stared down at his hands and didn't say anything, so I said, 'Well, Dad, you're not jumping to say no, here, so I'm gonna assume that's a yes.' You guys can stop lying to me now, Mommy. I *know* Daddy had an affair."

What I did next, I will regret for the rest of my life. I said to Avery, "Don't say anything to your father about any of this. Don't get angry. Just play it cool." At the time, I felt that Mario was in a fragile state and I didn't want to deal with any kind of white rage from him after Avery had gone back to school. I just wanted to contain the situation because I felt like his behavior was so erratic. I was scared and I was weak. So I basically asked my daughter, who had just told me that she had found out that her father was not the man she thought he was, not to feel what she had a right to feel and not to express what she had a right to express. I remember right before Avery left for school, we all went out for her last dinner in the city. The three of us sat there making small talk and she had to pretend that was everything okay, because that's what I asked her to do. She hadn't spoken to Mario since their conversation in her room. No one addressed the elephant in the room and, because she loves me and she loves her father, Avery agreed to play along. She was never allowed to lose it and be angry, which wasn't healthy for her. After that, Avery actually put herself in therapy because I would call her crying and she told me Mario would call her crying. She was only seventeen years old, and she was playing mediator to her parents. I am so grateful that she has a strong sense of self and that she has come through this without becoming jaded or bitter.

The next day, Mario drove Avery to the airport and when he got back we met for breakfast. I said to him, "Mario, I left some bags out for you. You need to pack your stuff up and you need to leave."

I remember, him being in shock and saying, "Please, don't do this."

I said, "I can't be around you. I'm a wreck. I can't. I just can't."

My heart was broken. My body was destroyed. I was overmedicating to numb the pain. I was falling apart and I just needed some time to myself.

Once Mario moved out, and I no longer had the stress of seeing him every day, I started to regain my health. I was able to sleep at night. I began to feel more like myself and I stopped taking anxiety medication. Two weeks later, I contacted Mario and told him I thought we should go out to Southampton together. I was feeling stronger and healthier and thought we could go out there together and talk about him moving back in. I expected him to be receptive, but I remember that he said he wanted to go out there by himself because he needed some time alone. I decided to drive out to the house and surprise him anyway. Honestly, in the back of my mind, I did think there might be another woman there, but I just figured if that happened, I would calmly tell Mario to ask her to leave.

When I got to the house and he saw me standing in the doorway, he had this strange look in his eyes. I remember thinking, *he doesn't look right. His eyes don't look right. Something's weird here.* He asked me what I was doing there, but the way he was looking at me scared me. I panicked. I couldn't bring myself to say that I was there to work on our marriage, so I said something like, "Oh, I'm just here to get some contact lenses," and tried to move past him into the house. I remember, he put his hands on my shoulders and physically pushed me out of the house. Somehow, I was able to twist and duck under his arms, to move around him. As soon as I was inside, I knew there was a woman in the house. In *my* house. I could sense someone upstairs, looking down from the catwalk. I saw takeout from La Parmigiana in the kitchen and I remember thinking, *how could he order from our restaurant?* Things escalated quickly and

I called the police. They came out to the house and made a report. While they were questioning us, I was in one room and Mario was in another. I heard the policeman say, "Mario, you're gonna have to leave with your guest," and then I remember hearing this female voice whining, "Why do we have to be the ones to leave? We just drove for four hours." I would have laughed if it weren't so sad.

The police report should have been private, but someone leaked it to the press so once again we found ourselves the subject of ugly tabloid headlines. At that point I was in a state of shock. I was vulnerable and I felt that I needed to speak to a divorce lawyer just to get some information. What I really wanted was some kind of legal separation, but things escalated quickly and, on January 29, 2014, I filed for divorce. I realized the night before we were going to serve Mario with the divorce papers that things had snowballed and I wasn't ready for such a drastic and final step. I tried to stop it from happening, but it was too late. The wheels had been set in motion and there was nothing I could do. Who knows? Maybe if I hadn't filed for divorce, we wouldn't be where we are now.

• 8 •

Sliding Doors

AFTER SHE HAD SOME time to process what had happened, Avery wrote the most beautiful and heartbreaking letter to her father:

Dear Dad,

I'm writing to you again because I hope that, as your daughter, I will be able to get through to you—but I don't even know if I can at this point. You admitted to me that you have been reckless and self-destructive. You need to stop and fix your actions before you lose everything that is good in your life. I know right now you are unhappy with your life and yourself. You need to put your life into perspective. You live in New York City, one of the greatest cities in the world, and have a beautiful house in Southampton. I know that you are unhappy with your job, but it was your choice to take on that responsibility. You could have left and tried something else, but you didn't. You can't blame mom for your unhappiness. You had this job long before you met her. If anything, I would hope that you can see mom brought you the greatest happiness and love that you experienced—me, your only daughter. You have traveled the world and take vacations yearly. Do you know how many people can say they have this? It is a very small percent. Think about when we went to Africa, and we saw all those families with no shoes and clothes. People have to walk miles just to get water. You have a healthy daughter and a wife who loves you more than life itself. Mom has stood by you through everything . . . She sat by your bedside for six months when you were going through your depression. Even in October when the first article came out, she denied it to protect YOU. She did it to protect our relationship and your business. How could you sit there at dinner when you came to visit me during Parents Weekend, when I went on about how both of you could never do this to each other? You didn't even blink . . . We were a trifecta and you broke us. What you have done and are still continuing to do is now forever damaging. You have no one to blame but yourself. It's about time you stop acting like a teenage boy and take responsibility for your actions.

My father who would drag me to church every Sunday for thirteen years would never do this. My father who would tuck me in and pray with me before I went to sleep when I was a little girl would never do this. My father who has always put me first, would never do this. At this point what I decide and what Mommy decides is up to us. We have given you multiple chances. I don't want it to be this way, but you have given us no choice. You broke our hearts repeatedly. You told me you would do better and try to fix things before I left, but you have not done one thing to make anything better. You show no remorse. Where is the heartfelt apology to either mom or me? Where are the flowers and the cards? Where is any effort to show you actually care? If you don't want to do that for me fine, but at least please do it for mom. You owe her and your marriage some remorse and a real apology.

This whole thing is an embarrassment to Mommy and me, and you have not once thought about how it would affect us. I am ashamed of you. How can you possibly work on a marriage and still continue seeing another woman? That does not make any sense . . . I know you say that you have been angry with mom for a long time, and there are issues you have had that I won't understand. You know it was never her intention to hurt you. It was your fault for never speaking up to fix things. You then blame the TV show too, but who are you kidding? You love being on it . . . You say you hate our lifestyle, but you know you love going on vacations and being at our house in the Southampton. You are just lost and confused.

You claim that this is your way of getting back at mom for how she has hurt you over the years and that everyone has affairs. Do you realize how crazy that sounds? You try to make up excuses for everything you have done to justify your actions, but there is no possible justification for this. You have hurt Mommy and me beyond words. You have played with her mind for months. You have cried, telling me you pushed her too far past the edge and are afraid you will never get her back. You told me you never want to lose mom or me because we are the two most important people in your life, but you never tried to actually work on your marriage. Mom was there for months, knowing you were having an affair, and she still tried to work things out with you because she loves you so much. You may say you lost your love for her, but I don't believe that. Even if you are not in love with her, deep down you still love her and care about her.

Honestly, you don't even know what you want. You kept changing your mind with Mommy like a light switch. You told me that you don't even care about this woman, and you see nothing with her in the future. If this is the case, why would you keep seeing her and continue to damage your future with mom and me? How dare you bring her to our house that I grew up in in Southampton? We have endless memories in that home. That is the bed where you and your wife have slept for eighteen years. No sane husband would ever bring his mistress into his family

home. You know Mommy came to Southampton to tell you that you could move back in. She had every right to kick you out of the house and pack up your things. You destroyed her mental health. You never respected her wishes or space. You never gave the marriage a chance. One day you will reflect and realize how badly you messed up.

You knew we were in the public light. You knew once the article in October came out that you should have stopped. All of this is your fault, so stop blaming other people and trying to rationalize your thoughtless decisions . . . Do something for me now to fix things. I know that my real dad would see all of this. I know my real dad would be appalled and never forgive himself for how he disgraced and hurt the two people who love him more than anyone on this Earth.

You are my father, but you haven't been acting much like one. It is time for you to fix the damage. I need you to make changes and show an effort, even if you disagree. You need to show you care about us. We were the three musketeers, the three best friends. You and I had the best relationship. I see light at the end of this long dark tunnel, but it will take time. Please reflect as you read this letter a few times. I miss my dad. I hope that one day soon I'll have the dad I always thought I knew and put on a pedestal my whole life.

Love your one and only daughter,
Avery

The next few months were some of the darkest of my life. The experience of seeing my daughter suffer while my marriage was collapsing was more traumatic than the three years I spent watching my mother die of leukemia. After he read Avery's letter, it seemed like Mario wanted to try to make things work between us. As hurt as I was, I just wasn't ready to walk away from him. We decided to try going on some dates, and by March he had moved back into our apartment. We went back into marriage counseling, but the sessions were very tense because I felt Mario was being impatient with me. On March 14th, Avery was in town, and Mario and I celebrated our twenty-second wedding anniversary. We opened a bottle of champagne, drank a toast, and went out to dinner. He had made a reservation at Rosa, this very romantic Italian restaurant, but it was the saddest anniversary of my life. It was so awkward. We didn't kiss. We didn't hold hands. There was so much distance between us. But then the next day we went to the Metropolitan

Family selfie at The Metropolitan Museum of Art

Museum of Art with Avery and being together as a family felt so right. Avery published a selfie of us on Twitter and the press went crazy with stories of how I was back with my "estranged" husband.

It felt so good to be connected as a family, but that night Mario seemed to shift again. I remember at dinner he was throwing bills at me, saying I need to pay this bill and that bill. Later, Avery said to me, "That's your whole problem with Daddy. He's always throwing bills at you. He expects you to do certain things, but then he gets mad at you when you do. Daddy never stepped up to the plate. He says he feels like we left him hanging in the wind, but he never tried to be in it." That night I got angry with Mario and I remember him saying that the window was closing on us. How can the window close on a marriage of twenty-two years? I felt like he hadn't owned up to anything and that he hurt me for months and then was impatient with me when I was trying to heal.

In May, Avery and I decided to give Mario an ultimatum: cut off all ties or lose your family. I was done with all the back and forth. I felt like we would make a little progress, but then something would happen and we would fall even further back. Since I knew him so well, I could tell when he was pulling away because he was connecting with someone else. Mario agreed to change his phone number and I was determined to make things work this time. It was during this very tenuous and fragile period in my marriage that we filmed the Reunion episode for Season 6. At the time, Mario and I were in such a precarious place that I didn't feel like I could speak about our marriage or his infidelity and I had promised him that I wouldn't. When Andy Cohen questioned me, I shut down. I got defensive and refused to comment. I regret that now. I have always prided myself on being the type of person who speaks openly and honestly about all aspects of my life. I should not have allowed someone else's needs to dictate my behavior. I signed on to do a reality show and, even though what was going on in my life at that point was happening off camera, the collapse of my marriage was, and is, part of my reality.

For the rest of that summer we worked on our relationship. I felt Mario was connecting with me, we were going to counseling, and things were getting better. Then one night he was late coming home from work. I remember, he called to say he was at Grand Central station and was on his way home. Forty-five minutes later, he still wasn't home. It takes fifteen minutes to get from Grand Central to the Upper East

Side. When he finally got home, I remember him giving me some story about having to take the bus because the train was too crowded and when I questioned him about it he got very defensive, so I dropped the subject. I thought, *we're seeing the therapist tomorrow. I'm not going to upset the applecart right now.* I took a sleeping pill and went to bed.

In therapy the next day, I said, "So, Mario, have you seen that girl recently?"

I remember he said, "Why are you asking me that now when everything is great with us?"

I said, "I'm not saying things aren't good, but I am your wife and you are my husband. I'm allowed to ask the question."

Eventually, Mario did admit that he had met with her on the street. I remember he told me that she had contacted him because her father was ill, she was very upset, and needed to see him. I do believe that, up to that point, he really had been trying. Nevertheless, that was my breaking point. I just couldn't do it anymore. I began to feel that he was just not happy with himself and, if he wasn't happy with himself, how could he be happy with me, or anyone else for that matter? For months I had I tried to help him, tried to help us, but I felt like he just kept pushing me away.

On August 7, 2014, Avery helped me put up a post on Twitter announcing that I was moving on with my life without Mario. I was about to start filming a new season of *Real Housewives*. It was time for me to take back control of my life and begin a new chapter on my own. Ironically, it turned out to be the same day that Bravo aired the Reunion episode in which I had refused to answer questions about what was going on with my marriage.

Although we were separated and I was trying to move on with my life, Mario moved back into our apartment the following September. He stayed in Avery's room, but it was difficult to coexist like that. I felt like having him in my space while I was still licking my wounds was excruciatingly painful. Despite everything we had been through, I don't think Mario understood why I needed space. Once again, over the next few months he seemed to go back and forth between wanting to move forward with our separation and impatiently wanting me to take him back. I felt as if I had been emotionally abused for a year and I needed time to heal. But I couldn't bring myself to ask him to move out again at that point because his business, which had been in his family for three generations, was in serious financial trouble. I was worried that if he did not have some kind of stability he might have a breakdown.

That fall we started filming Season 7 of *Real Housewives* and I think Mario was hurt that he found out about it through the press. I remember we argued about my filming in the apartment. I thought it would help if he had a place of his own, but when I told him that I had looked at an apartment for him it only seemed to upset him more. For the first time it occurred to me that Mario felt that the show had ruined our marriage. When *The Real Housewives of New York City* came into our lives, Mario and I were both at professional crossroads. I had a seven-figure business, but after twenty years of running my own company I was starting to feel burned out. Although I was successful, I was open to change and ready for a new challenge. At the same time, because its lease was up, Mario's company had

The Berkshires, Season 7

At the airport with the ladies on the way to Turks and Caicos

recently moved locations, which shook things up and made him unhappy. Meanwhile, things in his line of work were becoming Internet based. In order to keep up with the times I had been encouraging him to develop a website. The main reason I initially agreed to do the show was that I thought it would help showcase that website. I wasn't looking for fame or fortune. I was making great money and I was happy with my life. I think at first Mario loved being on the show with me. He wrote animated and entertaining blog entries commenting on the show and even took the spotlight in a couple of episodes when he went toe-to-toe with Jill or LuAnn. Although I wasn't looking for it, the show opened up so many doors for me and, being the ambitious businesswoman that I am, I took those opportunities and turned them into one success after another. As I became more

Avery's first birthday

successful on the show, I think Mario began to feel that he was fading into the background, that I wasn't being a team player anymore, and that I had somehow left him behind. Ironically, the very thing I did to help my husband, he now seemed to feel had ruined our marriage.

Mario and I have been through so much together. Over the course of two decades, we raised a child together, traveled the world, built two homes, and supported one another through all four of our parents' deaths. But once I started doing the show my life began to move in one direction and his in another. The underlying foundation of our marriage began to shift, and I didn't realize he was unhappy until it was too late. Most men define themselves by success. Even if the man isn't the dominant one in the marriage, I think it must be emasculating if the wife's multiple businesses are successful while the husband's business is falling apart. I remember Mario used to always say that his business was like a clock; it would never make a lot of money but it was always very consistent. Until it wasn't. I think he must have been overwhelmed by all the problems and couldn't see a way out. I have always told Mario that I don't think a man's worth is measured by his financial success. We run with a very affluent crowd and I've known women who are married to billionaires and they are still miserable. If a friend showed me a twenty-carat ring her husband had given her, I never felt jealous because I always felt good about myself and was happy in my marriage. Being a billionaire does not make you a good husband or father, but I think Mario got so caught up in striving for a certain lifestyle that he lost sight of that.

A year after the story of Mario's affair broke in the press, we did come close to reconciling. He called me on my birthday in November, sang "Happy Birthday" to me, and told me he wanted to make our marriage work. There were moments where we would connect and I would soften towards him. I could almost see a light at the end of the tunnel for us, but ultimately I began to realize that he was still going through whatever it was that had caused him to stray outside our marriage in the first place. Even though he said he wanted to work things out, it didn't feel like he was putting any energy into the marriage. I had reached the point where I couldn't be with him if I didn't feel like he had the energy to make it work. Maybe we would have had a chance to save our relationship if he hadn't kept moving back into our apartment while I was still healing. I think it was too much pressure on both of us. Looking back, I don't believe Mario was ready to really work on our marriage. I'm not sure he ever will be.

When you're with someone for more than twenty years, he or she becomes part of you. I had been with Mario almost my entire adult life and walking away from our marriage has been the most painful thing I have ever had to do. Mario and I always had passion, we always had love, and we were always simpatico. For more than two decades we walked side by side, in perfect step with one another. His thought was my thought. His heart was my heart. Even now, with all the stress and the pain we've been through, he is still the love of my life. How do you separate from someone who's a part of you? It's like taking Siamese twins and ripping them apart.

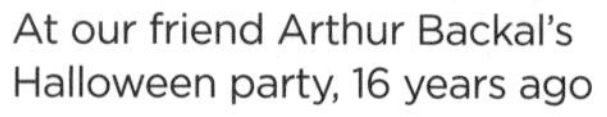

At our friend Arthur Backal's Halloween party, 16 years ago

Cooper's Beach, Southampton

Over the past year when he was ready to come home, I wasn't ready to take him in. When I was open to resolving things, he would retreat. We are like sliding doors; the opportunities come and go but we never connect. It's not the first time we've been in that place. We very nearly missed the opportunity to be together at all. Before I was engaged to the doctor, we had gone out on one date. We had a great time and were very attracted to one another, but somehow we got our wires crossed. We had planned for our second date that Mario would take me out on his boat.

He had said, "Ramona, I'm gonna pick you up on Saturday. Take a change of clothing, we'll go on my boat and then we'll go for dinner. I'll call you early Saturday morning."

That Saturday I waited for his call, but by eleven o'clock my phone still hadn't rung. I figured he was probably in bed with some chick from the previous night. The longer I waited the more worked up I got. I thought, *how dare he stand me up like this?* So I called him up. When he answered the phone his voice was hoarse and he sounded congested.

"I'm really sick, Ramona. I'm sorry I didn't call you. I was hoping I'd feel better," he croaked.

I totally thought he was making it up, so I just said, "That's okay. Feel better," and hung up.

Two days later he left me a message, "Hi, it's Mario. Call me."

That's it. Just, *hi, it's Mario. Call me.* My sister's reaction was, "What kind of message is that?" We both said that he should have at least apologized for standing me up. So I never called him back. I found out later that he was upset with me because he really was sick and I never called him to check up on him to see how he felt, which was why his message came off a little cold. We each have a different interpretation of why our second date never happened, but the one thing we can both agree on is that the chemistry between us was powerful. After that, we both got sidetracked by other relationships for a while, but we'd run into each other at the gym from time to time and flirt. When we finally reconnected a few years later it felt like fate. The day that Mario called me out of the blue to ask me out again, my life changed forever. For the first time in my life I knew it was possible to be in a loving, supportive relationship.

I loved Mario more than I could have ever imagined possible. He was my lover, my partner, and my best friend. For most of our marriage he wasn't intimidated by my success; in fact he was always very proud of my endeavors in business. I remember he would joke, "Ramona, you know how to bring home the bacon and fry it up in a pan." I always felt like he loved that I knew how to make money *and* be a homemaker. He had always been totally and unconditionally supportive, but I think once he turned sixty something in him must have snapped and suddenly he began to see my success differently. By that point, his business had been struggling for years and I think that had chipped away at his self-esteem. Meanwhile, I was busy branching out in different directions. I was becoming more successful, and spending more time away from home. Even though there was no way I could have foreseen the impact on my marriage, there was a part of me that was apprehensive about starting the wine business because I was already so overextended with my other businesses and with filming for the show. I remember at one point I even said to Mario, "I don't know if I should do the Pinot." I think more than the show, it's the Pinot that really destroyed my marriage. I was filming for five months of the year and then for another five months I was on the road every week, as well as traveling one week every three months for HSN. On top of all that I was raising my daughter, helping her get into college, running two homes, doing charitable work, and being social. I loved doing the Pinot. I still do, but it was all-consuming and for a while it took over my life.

I was talking to a friend recently who said that people step outside the marriage because something has already broken down from within, sometimes even years earlier. I'm very strong and outgoing. I know what I want and go after it. I'm direct and I speak my mind, but I'm not always sensitive to other people's feelings. Mario is the polar opposite. He's very warm and sensitive, but he can also be very passive and uncommunicative. Initially, that was what drew us to one another. For years we balanced each other out, but somewhere along the way, the thing that made us work became the very thing that was tearing us apart. I think I became too strong for him and he began to resent me for it. I've asked myself over and over how, after twenty-plus years, we fell apart so quickly and painfully. I think the real reason our marriage failed is that we had a breakdown in communication. It boils down to the simple truth that I wasn't attuned enough to his needs and he wasn't articulating how much he needed. Resentment built up until finally it broke us.

I believe that when a spouse strays outside a marriage of many years, more often than not, it's not usually about the partner. I think it comes from a place of deep unhappiness and instead of communicating with their partner, the spouse goes looking outside the marriage for something to make him or her feel whole again. My advice to anyone who is contemplating stepping outside a marriage because he or she thinks a connection with someone else will fill that void, is to first go to your partner and communicate by saying, *I don't feel good about myself. I don't feel good about us. Can you talk to me? Can you hold me? I need special attention.* An affair is a quick fix, but it is not a solution. The underlying issues that caused you to behave in a self-destructive way will still be there and now you have dragged your family down with you. Try counseling or at least make time for a quiet dinner together. In marriage, even if there's still passion and there's still love, it's easy to fall into living parallel lives. Unless one person says, *I'm in pain right now,* the other person has no way of knowing and can't help. Once communication breaks down, wounds will fester and even the strongest marriage can fall apart.

Of all the things I've been through this is by far the most painful. I used to think the hardest thing was watching Mario deal with his anxieties about his company. I remember waking up in the middle of the night, thinking my life was a nightmare because my husband was so upset and couldn't get out of his own head. But at least then I felt that he still needed me; at least he was there by my side and he would say, *I love you* and *thank you for supporting me*. I think maybe the reason why I stayed in this relationship longer than most women is because I don't like to fail at anything and the last thing I ever want to do is fail at my marriage. This is the hardest thing because I don't understand it. I wish I could fix things but I can't. I actually said to Mario in therapy once, "I wish I could take away all your pain." If I could, I would take in all of Mario's pain because I had always loved him so much.

I believe if his business were doing well, we'd still be happily married. It's not like Mario and I haven't endured tragedy. I think it was only when his self-esteem began to deteriorate that we started to fall apart. Looking back, I think he was in the midst of a midlife crisis. It can happen to anyone, male or female, and it is often triggered by such factors as a child leaving home or a struggling or failing business. These potentially traumatic life events can result in an overall sense of dissatisfaction within oneself, which can last for two to six years.

I feel such sadness that I have lost my partner and my

best friend. When I think of life beyond my marriage, it's very discouraging. I'm not so much worried about meeting someone else since there are plenty of men out there. It's more about finding a soul mate and having a deep connection with someone with whom you want to spend the rest of your life. If I want to be in a relationship again, I am going to have to learn to be softer. I'm a strong, independent woman and that's intimidating to a lot of men. One of the best things about Mario is that he loved me for me and I never had to pretend to be someone I wasn't.

I believe that things happen for a reason and that maybe this has been some kind of a blessing in disguise for me. Maybe Mario and I fulfilled our roles in one another's lives and there is a better life waiting for me in the future. For many, many years we had a great marriage and together we raised a beautiful daughter, who has grown into an intelligent and ambitious young woman. Maybe we just outgrew one another. We see the world so differently now. I feel like Mario wants to sell both of our homes and retire. To me, that's unthinkable. He's only sixty-two; he's going to live for another thirty years. I feel like he lost his purpose in life and I don't believe selling our homes and retiring will make him happy if he has no direction. I can't imagine being with someone who doesn't want to work for the next thirty years. I don't care how much money I have, I will always want to be involved with something and will never have too much idle time. I still have as much ambition and energy as I did when I was thirty—maybe more. I need to feel motivated and mentally stimulated. I feel that Mario gave up on himself, on his business, and on us. I think somewhere along the way he got lost. I tried to help, but you can't help someone who doesn't want to be helped. That can only come from within.

I draw strength from knowing that I was a good wife and that I did try to make my marriage work. I know that some women might think that if their husband had sex with another woman they would dump him that day. To that I can only say, easier said than done. You can't judge me until you have lived in my shoes, until you have been married for over twenty years to a man who was always a good husband and a good father. People have indiscretions; they can fall off the cliff, and sometimes you have to try to forgive.

I myself have been guilty of judging other women. I made comments on the show that I can now see were hurtful because they were based on ignorance. Now that I have gone through a painful separation myself, I realize that I should have been more understanding of the women in my life who have gone through a similar experience. Both Sonja and LuAnn went through painful separations and looking back, I see that I could have been more supportive. The first time I saw LuAnn on camera while we were filming Season 7, she was having an estate sale to sell off the furniture from the home she shared with her ex-husband because she had bought a new house in Sag Harbor and was ready to move on. I went over to her and took her off to the side. I told her that I wanted to say something to her and that she didn't have to respond if she didn't want to. I said that I wanted her to know how sorry I was for the way I behaved and the things I said to her when she was having problems with her marriage and going through her divorce. She told me she appreciated my apology, but I think she was reluctant to let her guard down with me at first. The proof is in the pudding, so to speak. Over the course of filming Season 7, a true friendship evolved between LuAnn and I and we have been very supportive of one another. I am so grateful to all the women on the show for supporting me through this dark period of my life. Without their friendship and continued support, I would never have been able to handle what I was going through.

I do believe in forgiveness, but it's difficult to forgive people who can't accept responsibility for the harm they have

Real Housewives of New York, cast of Season 7

Last day of shooting, Season 7

caused you. I feel like I have been Mario's punching bag and that he has blamed me for everything that was wrong with our marriage and his life. I don't think he has ever truly been willing to take responsibility for his actions. Although it may have been a symptom of his unhappiness with himself and our marriage, it is not my fault that he had an affair. I've read that when one partner has an indiscretion and betrays the other partner—because sometimes it's the man and sometimes it's the woman—it takes a good two years to repair the damage. I would be willing to put in the work, but I don't believe that Mario is capable of that kind of sustained self-reflection. I think he's too fragile.

Obviously, Mario and I have to come to some sort of resolution, but at this point it's more financial than emotional. It's sad that twenty-plus years of marriage can be reduced to a distribution of assets in the blink of an eye. We were a two-income family and, because of my business I was able, with Mario's support, to earn the money we needed to acquire our two homes. I think Mario wants me to agree to sell both of our homes, but I want to keep the house in Southampton. I've been in our condo on the Upper East Side for nineteen years. I don't know what's going to happen, but I'm looking at apartments in the city now to see what's out there in my budget. Maybe it's time for a change. I don't think Mario understands why I want to hang on to the Southampton house, though. I think to him it's just a roof and four walls that have a set financial value, but to me that house is so much more. Avery and I have so many memories there. It's painful to think of losing that house. I have always believed that the three things in life you need to be happy are your partner, your career, and your home. I've lost all three before and I was able to rebound and now I find myself in that place again. I have lost the love of my life and my career and businesses are in flux, but I don't want to lose my homes as well. At this point in my life, the idea of rebuilding from scratch is overwhelming.

Thankfully, Avery has come through all of this with her spirit intact. I always tell her how proud I am of the amazing young woman she has become. Avery can be very hard on

Me and Avery in happier times at our home in Southampton

herself, especially about schoolwork. I remember during that very stressful year, when she came home for winter break, she was beating herself up about her grades. I took her hand and told her, "Avery, getting all As doesn't matter. You are so unbelievably special and smart. I know that in life you will succeed in a huge way." Despite all the pain she endured, she worked hard all semester and got herself into the University of Virginia. She is in love with her school and is finally having a true college experience. I've visited her there and agree that it's the perfect place for her. Avery has taken me with her to frat parties and we have become closer than ever this past year. She has become as much my friend as she is my daughter. We see UVA as a gift for her after all the pain she has been through. Finally, my daughter is happy again.

I don't know what the future holds for me. For the first time in my life I can't see where the road ahead leads.

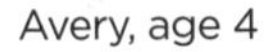

Avery, age 4

Me and Avery, August 2014. Our first night alone together in Southampton after Mario and I split for good

Maybe that's why this is happening. Maybe my challenge right now is to embrace the uncertainty of life. Every day is a struggle and there are times when I still can't believe this has happened to us. What gives me the strength to go on is my faith in God. I pray to God every day for myself, for Avery, even for Mario. Because of everything I have been through, I know that am strong enough to handle anything life throws at me. I have always been independent, always stood on my own two feet. Whatever happens with my marriage, I know that I will be okay. I've learned that you just have to face whatever life throws at you head on. Some days I feel strong, other days not so much, but I wake up every morning and put one foot in front of the other until I find that I am moving forward.

Whenever things feel hopeless, I hear my mother's voice, *you must have faith in God, Ramona, and you must have faith in yourself. Always know that if you have faith, true faith, you can accomplish anything*. Despite everything she went through, my mother never gave up and neither will I. Life is a roller coaster, or in my case it's a Ramonacoaster. Sometimes it's thrilling, sometimes it's terrifying, but you just have to raise your hands in the air, throw your head back, and enjoy the ride.

ACKNOWLEDGEMENTS

FIRST I WOULD like to thank all of my fans for the love and support over the years and this most difficult recent journey.

To my mother: Through her I became the strong independent woman I am. She taught me to be directed and positive and that I could attain anything in my life.

To Mario: I thank you for being a great husband and father for so many years. Through your love and support I accomplished so many things.

Avery, you have been my shining light through some of my darkest moments. I look at you and see a young woman who is as beautiful inside as on the outside. You have wisdom beyond your years. You have a great soul, heart and such compassion. The love I have for you surpasses anything I thought possible. You inspire me to embrace my new beginnings.

Thanks to my managers at NBTV Studios who have helped me through this exciting process.

Lastly, to everyone at Bravo: The journey on RHONY has taught me so many things about myself.

And to Andy Cohen, who has given me his encouragement and helped me be me. . .